To Nobby David —

Our dear friend, and the unwitting model for p. 68 of this volume —

With much love,

Richard Ham

THE COMPLETE PIANIST
BODY, MIND, SYNTHESIS

by
Ruth C. Friedberg

The Scarecrow Press, Inc.
Metuchen, N.J., & London
1993

The illustrations in this book were drawn by Dr.
Samuel J. Friedberg.

British Library Cataloguing-in-Publication data available

Library of Congress Cataloging-in-Publication Data

Friedberg, Ruth C., 1928–
        The complete pianist : body, mind, synthesis / by Ruth
  C. Friedberg.
            p.   cm.
        Includes bibliographical references.
        ISBN 0-8108-2630-5 (acid-free paper)
        1. Piano—Instruction and study. 2. Piano—
  Practicing—Physiological aspects. 3. Piano—Perfor-
  mance. I. Title.
  MT220.F83   1993
  786.2' 19—dc20   92-39275

Manufactured in the United States of America

Printed on acid-free paper

To my teachers, my students, and my colleagues,
and to the art we serve

CONTENTS

Contents

LIST OF ILLUSTRATIONS

PREFACE, BY LORIN HOLLANDER

The Complete Pianist: Body, Mind, Synthesis is a remarkable piece of work by an equally remarkable teacher, philosopher, and healer. Ruth explores with wonderful clarity and thoroughness virtually every important aspect of the mind, heart, body, and soul of the creative person. This is truly a book for our age, and would make valuable reading for those pursuing most fields of human endeavor.

Lorin Hollander

AUTHOR'S PREFACE

The word "pianist" conjures, in many minds, a cartoon-like vision of ten highly mobile fingers mysteriously connected to a brain. It is not the author's intent to erase this vision, but rather to dispel the mystery of the connection.

The question then becomes, what exactly is the role of the body in establishing, helping, or hindering the pianist's process, and, further, how can the mind's unending activity be harnessed most effectively to facilitate this process.

By this point in the late twentieth century, performing musicians, along with the rest of society, are reaping the fruits of extensive "body work" as purveyed through many advocates and systems, as well as of new psychological insights into learning and how it operates. We will explore those areas of this information which seem to the writer to be most relevant to the pianist, and will supply, for further study, extensive annotated bibliographies of books and periodicals published during the past fifty years.

In the final section of the book, the ultimate synthesis of musical activities of the body and mind, which is known as "performance," will be investigated. Throughout, words of advice from the great pianists and pedagogues of our time will be included when pertinent to the subject at hand.

In some cases, bibliographical references will be applicable to more than one of the book's major divisions. These will either be listed in more than one place if equally relevant, or following the section to which they primarily pertain. Readers will usually be made aware of the multiple relevancy by careful attention to the annotations.

Readers will also observe that that the generic "he" has been used in many places where both sexes are clearly included. This has been done for the sake of brevity only and the reader is assured that *all* pianists-male or female, short or tall, fat or thin, solo or ensemble-are herein addressed.

Ruth C. Friedberg
San Antonio

INTRODUCTION: THE MAKING OF A PIANIST

This small book on a large subject was written in response to student requests and is a distillation of many years' concert and teaching experience. It is intended to serve piano students, teachers, and performers as a handbook of useful advice to be consulted at many stages along the path to becoming a pianist.

Since anyone who purports to speak from experience had better be prepared to describe it, what follows is a brief history of my pianistic life. It is, in many ways, atypical, and may serve to suggest that each pianist's pathway toward and into his life's work assumes a unique pattern, adapted to the individual's physical and psychological endowment.

I was born in Atlantic City, New Jersey (long before the advent of the casinos), and began to study the piano at the age of seven. Although my first teacher's grasp of the advanced literature was somewhat limited, she gave me two important gifts: an extensive grounding in scales, Hanon, and Czerny, and her insistence that my parents purchase, at the outset, a brand new Steinway baby grand with which I immediately began one of the major love relationships of my life.

As my technical abilities were developing, I also started to demonstrate a capacity for sight-reading that helped to determine the eventual direction of my musical career. At the age of eleven, I was invited to play in the junior high school orchestra, and subsequently became accompanist for my high

school glee club. Already comfortable in large group performance, I gradually came to realize how much pleasure I
derived from solo accompanying and chamber music, and was
soon performing with individual singers from the glee club
and as a member of the official high school piano trio.

All this time I continued to study and practice the solo
repertoire, and although my high school grades qualified me
to be a class graduation speaker, I elected (having been given
the choice) to perform two Chopin etudes at the ceremonies.
At the strong urging of my original piano teacher, I had
sought a new teacher in my junior year of high school, and had
begun to travel every Saturday to Philadelphia to study with
Martin Lisan. This proved not only beneficial to the broaden-
ing of my pianistic repertoire, but occasioned a quantum leap
in my overall artistic development. I now had weekly access to
all the resources of a great city, and after spending an always
enlightening hour with Lisan in his studio at 17th and
Chestnut Streets, I would often visit museums, and end the
day with a concert at the Academy of Music or Robin Hood
Dell (depending on the season).

Having had, since childhood, a strong academic bent, and a
great love of literature and language, I was wary of the
over-specialization of conservatory life and indeed, because
of the smallness of my hands, was not initially convinced of
my fitness for a pianistic career. I therefore chose a liberal arts
college, Bryn Mawr, in Pennsylvania, and started my college
work as a political science major. I continued to study piano in
Philadelphia, however, practiced early every morning before
classes began, and became the accompanist for the Bryn Mawr
College Chorus. This choral group had the good fortune to be
directed at that time by Lorna Cooke DeVaron, who encouraged my growing sense that I should be involved with music
professionally. At the end of my sophomore year, we both left
Bryn Mawr (which did not offer a music major until several
years later). "Cookie," as we called her, went off to forge a

distinguished career at the New England Conservatory, and I enrolled as a music major at Barnard College in New York City.

Going to school at Bryn Mawr had provided me with the opportunity to continue absorbing the rich musical life of Philadelphia. I attended a regular Monday night orchestra series at the Academy of Music and was also introduced to the glorious sound of the string quartet in an evening whose impact on my musical senses I shall never forget. Now, in New York, the possibilities were almost overwhelming. I heard traditional opera at the Met, the Juilliard Quartet from the stage of Carnegie Hall, Marie Powers on Broadway in *The Medium,* the opening of Rodgers and Hammerstein's *South Pacific*, and so on in a seemingly endless list.

Great music was all around me, and I was extremely fortunate as well in my instructors. Frank Sheridan, teaching piano at Barnard as well as the Mannes School, helped me establish what I could do most successfully on the piano with my barely-an-octave span. Jacob Avshalomov, later of Portland Youth Orchestra fame, taught me counterpoint. I learned music history from Abram Loft, who was to become second violinist of the original Fine Arts Quartet, and had other exciting classes in music literature with Carolyn Cady and Otto Luening. My one regret was not being able to schedule a course with Douglas Moore, whose inspiring presence on the faculty of Columbia University (where Barnard students had most of their music classes) set the tone of the whole program.

Although performance was not required for my Barnard Bachelor of Arts degree with a music major, I continued to study the solo literature with Sheridan and to seek out and play with singers and other instrumentalists. Fortuitously, I found a violinist in the mailroom whose mail was regularly mixed with mine since we shared the same last name. We began to concertize together, with the occasional addition of a horn player from Juilliard, which at that time was still located just a few blocks down Broadway from Barnard and Columbia.

With Martin Lisan I had begun to discover the greatest works of the piano literature and become inspired to attempt my own projections in performance of their profound message. With Frank Sheridan, I learned how much detailed work and precise study of scores was required for the full realization of these grand projections, and I started to imitate his meticulous care in fingering and pedal indications. By the time I left college, I had also studied three languages (French, German and Spanish), philosophy, history, Shakespeare, and European painting, and felt that I had made a good compromise between advanced piano studies and a firm liberal arts grounding.

At this point I married and moved back to Philadelphia, where my husband was in medical school. Losing no time, I presented myself at the New School of Music , which was run by the Curtis String Quartet, with Max Aronoff as its director. I was soon studying with Vladimir Sokoloff who helped me fill in some gaps in my knowledge of the solo literature, and guided me in the ensemble performing experiences that were increasingly coming my way. The New School of Music, which sponsored the New Chamber Orchestra at that time, was a performers' school, and I was soon asked to be part of the New School piano trio, in which capacity I concertized in the Philadelphia and mid-Atlantic area. I was constantly in demand to accompany singers on the many school recitals and around town, all of which was steadily building my repertoire in the vocal and chamber music literature.

The New School of Music also accorded me my first teaching opportunities, for, solely on the basis of my Barnard degree (since I had no experience), I was asked to give piano lessons to beginning students, and theory classes to returning World War II veterans. As is so often the case, I learned almost as much about the piano in teaching others how to play it as I had in my own studies. Although I had set out to be a performer, not a teacher, I began to see that the two could be rewardingly combined.

Several years into this first phase of my professional life, I experienced simultaneously the two greatest career hazards of young women: the birth of a child and an enforced family move. My husband and I first returned to Atlantic City for his internship, and soon thereafter left with our son for Parris Island, South Carolina, where he was to be stationed for a two year stint as a Navy doctor attached to the Marine Corps.

Looking back, I realize that this was a crucial period in my life, when I could easily have despaired of my musical future and let my pianistic skills deteriorate to the point of no return. As the reader will quickly surmise from the existence of this book, I did not do that. I now owned my beloved Steinway which my parents had given me several years before, and, in the absence of the musical colleagues I had grown used to, I determined to practice the solo repertoire daily during my son's early afternoon nap. The depths of my chagrin on the day he discovered how to leave the crib unaided was exceeded only by my joy in realizing that I could play even with a child "on the loose," and so began our mutual liberation.

Interestingly, the tiny town of Beaufort, South Carolina, which was long on the beauties of the Old South but short on cultural stimulation, did eventually yield a musical colleague of sorts. She was an amateur pianist, originally from New York, now married to a local doctor and as hungry as I was for artistic communication. We played the four-hand literature as often as we could and bolstered each other's recollections of the musical worlds we had known.

As it happened, coming out of the Service did not return me to the Northeast, nor have I ever returned there as other than a visitor. My husband decided to enter the residency program at Duke University in Durham, North Carolina. Within a few months of our move, I was involved in a flurry of musical activity, playing with any number of singers and instrumentalists from the Duke community and music faculty. As it became apparent that my husband would choose to stay in academic medicine, I decided to prepare myself to teach on a college level, and earned an M.A. in musicology at the University of North Carolina which was in Chapel Hill, just a short ten miles from home.

Once again, I had chosen an academic rather than a performing degree. One of the reasons for this was that my performing skills and proclivities had been solidifying over the past decade to those of an ensemble pianist, and in those days there were no programs established to confer degrees in this area. In a way, I was already involved in advanced ensemble training in the work I was doing with the Duke music faculty and students, which was increasing my knowledge and command of the vocal and chamber repertoire by geometric progression, as it seemed. Furthermore, because of my continuing attachment to literature and writing, I welcomed the possibilities for research that the musicological studies would afford.

Teaching opportunities had also resurfaced soon after our arrival in North Carolina. I returned to giving piano lessons, now not only to children but also to adults, for whom I was discovering a particular pedagogical affinity. By the time I had completed my master's degree, I was offered a position, first part-time and soon full-time, on the Duke music faculty. This proved to be a happy combination of performing duties as staff accompanist, and classroom teacher of everything from ear-training and music literature courses, to the coaching of piano students in the vocal and instrumental ensemble literature in which I had become a specialist.

Still another rewarding aspect of my Duke appointment was the opening up of a new performing area. With a fine fellow faculty pianist, I formed a two-piano team, and concertized extensively as part of this duo in recital programs and as concerto soloists with the Duke Symphony Orchestra.

It was at Duke, also, that my career in musical journalism began to blossom. I had articles on twentieth-century piano music and vocal literature published in several leading journals, and was invited to write on a number of American and British composers for the sixth edition of *Grove's Dictionary of Music*. It was, in general, a well-rounded and fulfilling life, and one which was difficult to leave when my husband's next career move took him to a new medical school, opening in San Antonio, Texas.

Despite my misgivings, however, Texas provided the nourishment for a further flowering of all of my work as a performer, teacher, and author. I had long wondered whether my pianistic skills would enable me to be employed solely as a performer at a high level of exposure. The answer came in a ten-year tenure as keyboard artist for the San Antonio Symphony during which I played everything: piano, celesta , and harpsichord parts within the orchestra; staging rehearsals and secco recitatives(on harpsichord) for the opera productions; solo roles in works such as Saint-Saens' *Carnival of the Animals;* accompanist to the symphony chorus, etc., etc.

During summer vacations from the symphony, I wrote and published a three-volume work on *American Art Song and American Poetry* (Scarecrow Press, 1981–87) which led to many appearances around the country as a lecture-recitalist. I also continued to publish journal articles, reviews of books and new music publications, and eventually even a collection of poetry with illustrations by my husband.

As always, my teaching as a vocal coach, pianist, and in the classroom continued: part-time while I was with the symphony, and full-time for the past five years at Incarnate Word College where I am now Director of Music. Of recent years, my ever-increasing work with many piano students at the college level has greatly broadened my conscious understanding of all the elements that go into the making of a pianist. I am glad to say that this a different book than it would have been had it been written even five years ago.

From this vantage point, and in full appreciation of the unique set of physical and mental characteristics and life experiences that each pianist possesses, I can wholeheartedly advise: "Use everything to your advancement. If you have small hands, become a Mozart specialist. If you have to move, find a new and more exciting job. From the raw materials of your body, your mind, and your life, carve your own inimitable and unsurpassable version of *The Complete Pianist*."

PART I   BODY

HOW WE SEE IT—OR DO WE?

The majority of performing pianists begin to study their instrument in childhood, or, at the latest, adolescence. Young bodies are, in general, without accumulated muscular strain, and for a number of years, the fingers and hands may be the only bodily parts the student recognizes as connected to his developing pianism.

In time, even his use of these vital structures becomes, and necessarily so, relegated to the realm of unconscious response. A honeymoon period of variable duration may then occur, during which the pianist glories in his increasing ability to be an effortless conduit between the notes on the page and the sounds that he brings forth. This is the time of "Look, Ma! No fingers!", when the player's performing process has become invisible to himself, and when there appears to be no intermediate step between musical apprehension and realization.

Unfortunately, the honeymoon, more often than not, ends as the player begins to perceive that his pianistic marriage is presenting some problems that were forming even in the very midst of his earlier raptures. Slowly he starts to notice that extended practice or rehearsal is attended by aching shoulders, headaches, or tension in the neck, and that even his precious hands and fingers may on occasion exhibit various symptoms of discomfort.

At the risk of overworking our metaphor, we may now contemplate the inherent justice of our pianist's punishment for failing to take his body with him into this intricate marriage. No longer able to be ignored, the body reasserts itself in the form of pain or disabling tension that interferes with the making of music. And only at this point perhaps, does a small gleam of understanding begin to grow that enables us to perceive our human bodily form as the vessel and medium of our talent, which must be cherished and nurtured with as much care and devotion as the talent itself.

HOW WE TREAT IT—PRINCIPLES
OF NURTURANCE

The life of a pianist is a strenuous one, requiring an unremitting daily expenditure of physical and mental labor. The pianist must indeed come to view his body much like that of an athlete in training, if he is to maintain his artistry through the many desired years of trouble-free performance.

Diet

Adequate nourishment is, of course, a basic principle. With the ever-increasing media attention to dietary information, we are all becoming aware of the importance of fiber and complex carbohydrates and of the deleterious effects of too much animal fat and refined sugar for those engaged in a largely sedentary occupation.

Another consideration which may be less obvious, however, is the value to a pianist of distributing his daily caloric intake over five or six smaller meals rather than three large ones. This serves the purpose of combating the fatigue factor inherent in long hours of practicing, rehearsing, and performing by providing at the same time both a welcome break period, and renewed fuel for the brain and muscles. It also lessens, and one might hope, will eliminate the need for constant caffeine and/or tobacco stimulation which can so easily create a debilitating cycle of dependence.

3

Rest

The precision and complexity of the pianist's daily level of muscular and neural functioning can only be maximally sustained by fully restorative periods of rest. Most of us are aware of what constitutes an adequate night's sleep, for although the necessary number of hours may vary between individuals, the sense of mental and physical well-being it confers on awaking is unmistakable. We are less aware, however, of the equal importance of rest periods through the working day. Our tendency is to stay on the piano bench to the point of pain or exhaustion when a well placed hiatus would probably have prevented the disability occurring in the short as well as the long-term picture.

Most symphony orchestra contracts mandate a break period after an hour to an hour and a quarter of rehearsal time. The principle followed here is a sound one. That is about as long as the body can comfortably sit with all faculties at attention, and prolonging the interval produces not only discomfort, but diminishing returns in the musical product.[1]

The message, therefore, is clear. If one is practicing, a time can easily be set for an hourly rise, accompanied by stretching or movement about the studio. Bella Davidovich, the great Russian pianist, is a devotee of this schedule. "I find that a one-hour period," she says, "is where I achieve the utmost in concentration. I work very intensively for one hour and then take a ten-, fifteen-, or twenty-minute break during which I will occupy myself with something completely different. . . . This method works so well that I can continue for eight hours, in one-hour periods, if there is time enough for that."[2]

If one is rehearsing with other musicians, all will benefit from a mutual time-out decision. If the pianist is accompanying singers, dancers, or opera staging, general breaks will usually be scheduled by the director, and should be used to incorporate a short walk or as much bodily movement as the situation allows. When a rehearsal situation is, for some reason, uncomfortably extended beyond the pianist's control, he can, while still "on the bench" unobtrusively rotate his shoulders, and roll his neck back and forth and side to side whenever possible.

The night's sleep and the day's rests, then, restore the brain and the body. But it is the vacation time that restores the creative spirit. In this writer's opinion, removing oneself totally from the area of one's accustomed musical activities has benefits which override the pianist's customary anxieties about diminishing skills when separated from his keyboard. The stimulation of new scenery, the time to read and contemplate , the opportunity to pamper the body with increased rest and motion, all serve to stimulate and develop the artist's inner resources on which he draws for the meaning of his performances. Here again, the scheduling is individual. Some require a week or two once or twice a year, some benefit from long weekend holidays, and others may need to spend a single day away from the piano on a more regular basis. Whatever his personal tempo, the pianist's life must emulate his musical apprehension of rhythmic patterning in which the pauses between are as important as the notes themselves.

Exercise

There is no way to overemphasize the importance, indeed the necessity, of exercise to a pianist, who must daily spend many hours pursuing his art form in a sitting position. Some abuse of this principle can be practiced with impunity in the earlier years when the body is young and flexible and excess more readily tolerated. But as time passes, it becomes ever clearer that exercise is a crucial factor in the pianist's release of muscular tension, maintenance of cardiovascular fitness, and the achievement of a sustained level of psychological well-being.

"But how can I exercise?" wails the busy performer. "I have barely enough time in my day to satisfy my teaching, playing, and practicing commitments, to say nothing of family and social obligations." To this, the only possible answer is that priorities must be set, lest one run the risk of accumulating physical and mental fatigue which can, in time, prove to be partially or totally disabling to the performer.

Fortunately, the patterns of our society have grown accustomed to allowing and encouraging the pursuit of fitness. The early morning riser will notice that he has much company as he performs his jogging stint before sitting down at the piano. If he prefers to finish his day with a relaxing swim or exercise class, he will discover that the majority of health clubs offer evening hours. And if he finds an exercise break during the day to be his most comfortable pattern, a brisk walk in the fresh air will serve equally well.

Concert touring or other forms of professional travel must not be allowed to serve as excuses for a disrupted exercise schedule. Sitting long hours in a plane, car, or bus can be more debilitating than sitting on a piano bench, and calls for compensatory types of movement as soon as possible after arriving at one's destination. The writer has discovered that present-day hotel and motel staffs are remarkably sanguine about guests making walking or jogging circuits around the property, and that in inclement weather, a surprising variety of calisthenics can be performed by spreading a towel on the floor in the privacy of one's room.

It is, of course, wise to avoid forms of exercise that may cause trauma to the bodily parts essential to the pianist's art.

Tennis, especially in the early stages of learning the game, can cause pain in the wrist and shoulder; skiing poses a potential threat to all four limbs; and other hazards abound in the more strenuous sports. Even ungloved gardening may menace the unwary in the form of cuts and insect bites (which usually occur, according to Murphy's law, one to two days before the next scheduled concert). Although swimming and walking are, overall, the most benign, ardent aficionados of other sports will continue to pursue them despite the hazards, and all that can be counselled is care and judgment. In the long run, the worst thing that a pianist can do about exercise, is not to do it!

HOW WE USE IT

Breathing

A generation ago, the subject of breathing would have been rarely if ever encountered in a book addressed to pianists. It is only in fairly recent history that we have come to recognize that the primacy of the breath in musical performance is by no means a principle restricted to singers and players of wind instruments.

Once we begin to pay attention to our breathing patterns, we become aware that muscular tensions are often associated with shallow breathing and breath-holding, and that conversely, relaxation and deeper, more rhythmical breathing also go hand in hand. "Through one simple exhalation," says Carolyn Grindea, "a performer gets all that is needed to counteract the effects of tension: the upper part of the torso becomes free, the back and neck are loose, the shoulders have dropped miraculously,. . . . the arm weight is transmitted to the hand and knuckles, while the fingers also receive a measure of the arm weight, supporting it, ready to pass it on to the keys. . . . If only more importance were given to freedom of breathing in piano playing (and in teaching), many of the problems created by tension would solve themselves.[3]

"Les pianistes," {those formidable beasts found in Saint-Saens' *Carnival of the Animals*} are the only musicians besides percussionists and other keyboard players who are not forced by the demands of their instrument to let the music breathe. Singers and wind-players must stop for air, while string players must change bow direction, and phrase shaping is calculated accordingly. Yet all of us have been subjected to the playing of pianists that went on and on in an unbroken, seemingly interminable stream of notes, with no gleam of light ever penetrating the breathless darkness.

The suggestion is frequently made to accompanists that they should "breathe with the singer", and for the most part this has been interpreted as the need to be aware of where the singer's breaths will fall in the vocal line for purposes of pianistic support and accommodation. If we examine the alternate interpretation, which would involve the pianist taking an actual breath when the singer pauses for this purpose, we find that this is not always desirable. The pianist's phrases, in an ensemble situation, are not always identical to the singer's or other instrumentalist's, and although he of course needs to maintain awareness of their patterns, his own may have different requirements.

A more helpful, overall suggestion for the solo or ensemble pianist is to breathe with the *music* {i.e. his own score}. This will have the effect of minimizing bodily tension, maximizing the flow of energizing oxygen, and assuring an adequate apprehension of rises and falls in the musical phrasing. Seymour Bernstein in *With Your Own Two Hands* describes useful breathing exercises to be done with the metronome in preparation for studying a new work. After concluding the exercises, the pianist is instructed to:

> Take a deep breath, and as you exhale, begin to play the music before you. In your expectant and unprejudiced state, you will respond naturally to the horizontal (melodic) and vertical (harmonic) structures, to the rhythmic patterns, and to all the marks of expression. Since the composition is new to you, the difficulties

cannot be anticipated. Thus, each musical event will inspire spontaneous feelings within you so that your muscles will adapt as naturally as possible to the physical movements necessary to express feeling. If you keep breathing with each phrase and remain receptive emotionally and physically, you will execute technical difficulties with surprising ease.[4]

Where the breath originates and its relationship to good body use are topics which will appear under subsequent headings. We must all remember that the breath is the life and carrier of the musical impulse, as it is the common thread of "line" in all the performing arts and in life itself. Stopping or ignoring its flow constricts our muscles and inhibits our musical meaning.

The Pianist's "Alexander"

F.M. Alexander was a turn-of-the-century Australian actor who, early in his career, began to have trouble with throat irritation and hoarseness while performing. The medical profession could not diagnose his problem, and so he embarked on a long, difficult period of detailed self-observation. In time, he became aware that misalignment of his head, neck, and torso brought on breathing difficulties, muscular tension, and vocal dysfunction. At this point he began a second career as a ground-breaking voice therapist and teacher. The basic principles of good body use which he developed proved invaluable to actors all over the world, and it was not long before singers and instrumentalists as well were discovering the "Alexander Technique."

Besides the purely physical aspects of the technique and, in fact, preceding their deployment, was a crucial psychological principle which Alexander gradually came to understand.

This was the concept of "inhibition", a word he used to refer to the conscious negation of the habitual bodily response to the *idea* of beginning a familiar activity. After a sufficient number of inhibitions, or saying "no" to the undesirable habits, he was able to consciously direct the formation of a new set of responses, and to point the way for all the generations of performers to come.[5]

The three primary tenets of the Alexander Technique, as it has come to be called, are these: the neck must be free and aligned with the spine, the head should be carried forward and up, and the torso allowed to lengthen and widen. These principles were, of course, originally applied to actors and singers in a standing position, bearing body weight on their legs. They can, however, apply equally well to pianists whose "sitting bones" are now serving as weight bearers.

In Alexander's view, the neck was the "primary control", and it is certainly true that a pianist maintaining involuntary tension in this area will almost predictably invite headache and shoulder strain. Holding the head in good alignment (the "second commandment") further reduces the likelihood of muscular strain, while lengthening and widening the torso allows the maximum space for rib cage expansion in the deep, rhythmic breathing which is the pianist's goal.

Not only does the Alexander Technique give us a picture of what good bodily use should look like on the piano bench, but it also prescribes restorative relief for the body during break-times. Practitioners recommend at least fifteen minutes a day to be spent lying on one's back on a firm, supporting surface with the knees up, feet flat, and head raised several inches (as by two or three small paperback books). This allows the spine to regain the length it has lost during the day's labors through compression of the vertebrae. It also affords an opportunity to practice muscular relaxation, deep breathing, and the concept of a fully extended torso while storing energy for the next practice session.[6]

Mirror, Mirror on the Wall

A well-placed mirror, which enables the pianist to view himself in profile, is an invaluable tool. This will enable the checking of the individual areas of the body for good use, as well as the gestalt of the overall physical involvement.

The first point of observation should be that the pianist's chair or bench is not too close to the piano and is of the proper height. Both these dimensions need to be adjusted so that the player's forearms are essentially horizontal to the keyboard, with the elbows slightly above the wrists. It is also necessary to have the feet planted firmly on the floor. If sitting well forward on the bench does not accomplish this, pianists with short legs may need to think about building up the underfoot area in some fashion, or wearing shoes with a heel high enough to compensate, but low enough for controlled pedaling.

Many pianists select a chair built with a full or partial back, which is especially useful for snatching rest periods in situations calling for long hours of playing. In any case, all pianists should sit well forward while playing, and must learn to use their lower abdominal and buttock muscles to support the torso, so as to prevent neck, arm, and shoulder strain. A useful concept in this connection is that of "released" muscles, a term used by Deborah Caplan to designate muscles which are contracting only enough to perform the required work, and with no added, gratuitous tension. Here is one exercise she suggests to develop this kinesthetic sensation of "release":

Pick up a cup as though you were going to drink from it. . . . Hold the cup close to your mouth and release as much tension from your neck, shoulder, and raised arm as you can without moving the cup. . . . What you just accomplished was releasing your muscles. You did not relax them, because they were still working to hold your arm up (muscles are relaxed only when they are not doing any work at all).[7]

The next gaze into the mirror focuses on our hands, and we hope to find that they do not exhibit the drawing up or tightness in the fourth and fifth fingers (the "tea-drinking syndrome") which lessens endurance and destroys control for numbers of performers. We check for gently curved fingers, wrists and arms fairly level with backs of hands, and an angle toward the keyboard that varies with changing technical demands. A constant, "frozen" hand position is neither possible nor desirable, and it must also be remembered that technique will always need to be adapted to the many varieties of shapes and finger lengths to be found in the individual hand.[8]

Another useful idea which mirror-gazing can help the pianist formulate sees the movement of hands on the keyboard as a kind of choreography, analogous to the movement of dancers' feet across a stage. Once established, this concept aids materially in the technical development of extensions, leaps, and the overall control of successive positioning of the hands with the greatest degree of planning and the least expenditure of energy. A further interesting analogy linking piano-playing to the art of the dance, an art in which all movement is generally conceived to be emanating from the center of the body, is the often quoted maxim of the famous piano pedagogue, Carl Friedberg: "You play from your stomach." What he is describing here, of course, is not an anatomical anomaly, but an intuitive sense of energy source, and the central focus for the gathering of bodily forces.

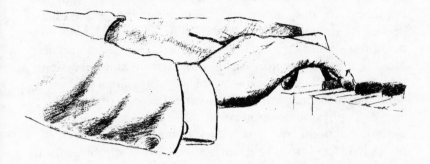

Figure 1. " The many varieties of shapes and finger length to be found in the individual hand."

Moving back from the hands, we observe the arm and shoulder for proper use of "weight transfer" (the now ubiquitous Matthay approach) when tonally appropriate.[9] Rodney Hoare, a student of Tobias Matthay's during the two years before the latter's death, has given us the following useful insight into this concept:

> I do not feel that Matthay advocated 'dropping the weight of the arms' on the keyboard in the manner of a dump truck unloading rubbish! However, he did advocate a whole arm touch from the *shoulders* when a large, full-bodied tone was desired. Unfortunately, this has often been overlooked. Subsequently, we see most weight playing from the wrist and forearm only.[10]

Next we view the full engagement of the wrist in up and down movement for wrist staccato playing, and lateral movement for full and half rotations. All finger, hand, arm, and shoulder movement will, of course, vary to some extent according to the musical demands of the period repertoire, and this will be addressed below in section three.

One hopes, however, that the position of the head will not be found to stray from its good alignment. Even in an orchestral situation, the head should not drop back from the neck, but should be carried back with the whole torso when looking at the conductor. Again, short stature may necessitate a higher bench or the carrying of a "professional cushion", which in turn may call for adjustment under the feet (see above). A physical position very similar to that assumed while watching a conductor occurs when coaching singers from the piano bench. Here, the gesture of throwing the head back while addressing the student must be abandoned in favor of merely raising the eyes.

A last observation in the mirror should take in the means employed to get closer to the keys when necessary or desirable. *Not* recommended in this context is dropping the head forward, and/or collapsing toward the keyboard. Highly preferable is approaching the keyboard with the entire torso as a unit, while pivoting from the hip joint.[11]

And On Arising

The pianist who determinedly maintains his "good use" (Alexander terminology) on the bench, only to get up and slump back to the rest of his badly aligned life, is certainly not fooling his body. For physical habits to persist and be maintained during the many—faceted stress of performance, a consistency of practice is required that pertains to all daily activities.

Once this realization has been achieved, the pianist will begin to observe how his head drops forward when he walks, how he sits in a contorted position writing letters at an uncomfortable table height, and how even the simple act of brushing one's teeth can present a challenge to good use of the body.

In the writer's experience, a series of private lessons or group workshops with a trained Alexander teacher can be a small investment yielding enormous dividends to the player's comfort and stamina, in performance and in daily living as well. One teaching encounter will not suffice. What is being described here is a kind of kinesthetic learning that must be constantly reinforced over a period of time, to enable the establishment of new neural and muscular patterns.

Other systems of "body-work" which may prove of general use to the pianist are Yoga and T'ai Chi Ch'uan, both ancient Oriental techniques which are becoming more and more widespread in the Western World. Yoga aims at a centering of the consciousness through deep breathing and a number of postures which provide gentle bodily stretching of muscles and joints.[12a12b] T'ai Chi Ch'uan is a series of slow, controlled, almost dance-like movements, which are likewise directed at achieving clarity, calmness, and balance.

The Yoga stretches are an excellent antidote to muscles fatigued from practice, and T'ai Chi principles have been recommended by some piano pedagogues for incorporation into the practice period itself. Gail Gross has described the relevance of T'ai Chi to pianists in these terms:

> "The most striking aspect of T'ai Chi Ch'uan is its endless seeming circular motion; circular energy that seems to accomplish much with little apparent effort. This circular motion is easily equated with what we consider 'rotational' movement as we play the piano. In T'ai Chi Ch'uan the circular motions unlock physical tension allowing energy to flow. The rotational movements at the piano keep muscles supple and prevent tense sounds."[13]

Gross goes on to suggest that all our solitary practicing can be experienced as a kind of meditation, and therefore as an end in itself, rather than merely as a *means* to an end. Courses in both Yoga and T'ai Chi are currently available on video tape, and classes are now becoming available in many cities throughout the United States. The techniques are worth investigating, as many performers can attest, for their potential contribution to our mental and physical health maintenance.

From Body to Mind

The majority of people in our contemporary society are quite familiar with the idea of the mind's power to affect the body. Discussion of psychosomatic disease is now a commonplace, and it has also become our expectation that mental/emotional states such as elation or depression will be transparently detectable in the lines of a face or the carriage of a torso.

Let us, however, consider for a moment that the opposite proposition may be equally true; that, indeed, a sagging, misaligned body may sap energy and generate depression, whereas a well-carried body, with a lengthening, supported torso, will *create* positive, energized responses throughout the consciousness. In the author's experience, the latter chain of events can definitely be induced, and the reason for this is apparently a mind-body connection so deeply intertwined that it can be activated from either end of the spectrum.

So we arrive at a paraphrase of the line from a well-known musical comedy hit which counsels "You may be as brave as you make believe you are". Our dictum would read "You may be as positive, confident, and relaxed as the position of your body and disposition of your features proclaim you are". This is crucial, of course, in establishing audience rapport from the first moment your public sees you step from the wings with easy shoulders, lengthened legs moving cheerfully and purposefully toward the bench, and an elegant, beautifully carried head. But it is of equal, perhaps even greater importance, when you choose, as you enter a room and sit down for a practice or teaching session, the message you will communicate to your colleagues in rehearsal, to your students, and, most particularly, to yourself.

NEW HELP FOR BODILY DISTRESS

Despite the pianist's resolve to maintain physical well-being, there are many among us who will find that, in the face of our best efforts, the cumulative effects of earlier bad habits or unavoidable stress of rehearsing and performing may cause dysfunction of the hands, fingers, or neck and shoulder area.[14] It should also be pointed out that pianists' hands, like singers' throats, seem particularly vulnerable to injury, for the dual reasons of highly specialized use, and increased focus of attention to the area.

The good news which follows this sobering prediction is that nowadays, much help is available to musicians suffering from the mildest to the most incapacitating physical performance problems. In a review article which appeared in the *New England Journal of Medicine*[15], Dr. Alan H. Lockwood traces the beginning of performing-arts medicine as a discipline, to the 1977 publication of *Music and the Brain,* a symposium of studies in the neurology of music.[16] In the years which have subsequently elapsed, this new specialty area has spawned a major journal called *Medical Problems of Performing Artists* (begun in 1986), a newly published *Textbook of Performing Arts Medicine*[17], and at least seventeen clinics in larger cities of the United States that are expressly dedicated to treating these problems.[18]

Dr. Lockwood directed one of these clinics in Houston, Texas, before a recent move to New York City. This writer had occasion to avail herself of its services in 1990 when seeking consultation on a non-performance-related hand problem. Dr. Lockwood, a professional neurologist and amateur musician, was found to have assembled a large group of physicians and therapists who brought their specialties to bear on the injuries and disabilities of performing musicians. Diagnosis was usually initiated by Dr. Lockwood himself, with the aid of an extensive history of the disability, and, when deemed useful, by observation of the musician in the act of performing.

In the author's case, the need for a minor surgical procedure at an early date was corroborated, and consultation with physical therapists specializing in hand work produced beneficial exercises for the interim period. The whole experience was extremely positive, not only because of the availability of disparate professional services in a single location, but also, and perhaps primarily, because of the patient being evaluated throughout the process in the context of a performing artist.

The new journal just described (*Medical Problems of Performing Artists*) offers many case studies of successful treatment similar to the writer's. Some cases are performance-related and others not at all. An example of the latter is a heartening discussion by physical therapist Gary Chleboun of a pianist who had inadvertently struck her hand against a car door and thereafter experienced an extended period of pain while performing. Following proper diagnosis of the problem, a series of mild stretching exercises for the right index finger enabled her prompt return to a full performance schedule. Such histories, we note gratefully, are becoming more and more commonly encountered.[19]

Why Does It Hurt?

At this point we need to address our attention to those disabilities which *are* related to our performance habits, in an effort to determine some of the sources of the problems and their possible solutions.

Teachers of the Alexander Technique are accustomed to being consulted by pianists who are experiencing tension and pain in the head, neck, and shoulders, or even in the arms, wrists, and hands. Eleanor Rosenthal, a San Francisco teacher of the Technique, who has written about it in both *American Music Teacher* and *Medical Problems of Performing Artists*, describes a pianist who came to her for help. Increasingly severe pain in the left elbow had made her totally unable to play, and Rosenthal's observation revealed excessive tension in the performer's arms, as well as a distinctive, habitual twist at the left elbow. Instruction in the Alexander principles of good total body use enabled a reduction of tension in the pianist to a point where she was able to resume a normal performance schedule after only two lessons.[20]

Unfortunately, the more zealous we pianists become in our search for perfection, the more it will likely elude us through the manifestations of increased tension. This tension was the habitual response that F.M. Alexander strove to avoid through his principle of "inhibition" (see above). Alexandra Pierce terms this same response "overdoing in performance", a syndrome which she describes as including "unnecessary movement, continuous and excessive muscular tension, and constant planning ahead."[21]

Pierce, who is a pianist, composer, and movement artist, has several suggestions for avoiding the pitfalls of "overdoing". The first is psychological, and involves staying centered in the present moment by relinquishing the conscious process of the ego and "thus making it possible to respond to the energy of the music with an outflowing of personal energy."[22] Her other suggestions are more physically oriented and are set forth in an excellent series of articles called "Pain and Healing for Pianists".

"The basic instrument of any musician is the body," says
Pierce. . . . "Musicians are specialized dancers. This proposition is clear enough to musicians when pain emerges. It may
be fingers that strike the keyboard, but troubles related to
playing emerge anywhere in our body."[23] She goes on to
suggest that maintaining the health of the musician's body
depends on its proper alignment and muscular support in
performance, so that sound may reverberate freely through
the body and down the spine in a "follow-through" effect that
promotes flexibility and release.

Artur Schnabel, one of the greatest pianists of the twentieth
century, outlined his view of the major causes of contemporary performers' physical stress in an interesting article
written for the now defunct *Etude* magazine. He pointed out
that, with the lighter actions of the earliest pianos, playing
could largely be localized in the fingers and hands, but that
modern-day, heavier actions demand controlled arm-weight
and the use of the whole body. This challenge, he adds, is
compounded by the fact that the hand is not naturally adapted
to keyboard-writing, because the most important parts (bass
and treble) fall to the weakest fingers (fourth and fifth). As
Schnabel puts it, "The necessity for playing forceful passages
in the soprano voice and the bass without stiffening the hand
or without cramped muscles, I consider the greatest technical
problem of modern playing."[24]

An Ounce of Prevention

Following the realization of Schnabel and others of how many
muscles are now used in piano playing and how extensively
they are employed, has come the new characterization of the
pianist as a special type of athlete. Practicing and performing
are now being compared to playing an athletic game, and
specific recommendations have been formulated by teachers

like Liz Manduca for warm-up exercises for the body and hands, relaxation and breathing techniques, the cool-down process, etc.[25] The rationale behind this new concept of pianistic "fitness" is, of course, to prevent trouble before it starts, by building and maintaining muscle tone and minimizing tension.

Although this approach seems relatively new, it was prefigured forty years ago by another great mid-century pianist, Andor Foldes, in an article called "It's All Done with Muscles". Herein, Foldes points out that playing the piano equals hiking or swimming as a muscle-builder, but insists that each pianist must develop his own physical equipment according to his individual needs and endowment.

> "[We must] fit the piano to the hand, not the hand to the piano", Foldes tells us, "[and] do away with old taboos about a fixed way of holding the hands and fingers. . . . Only the playing hand can determine what its own proper fingering shall be. . . . The sole test of 'right' fingering is whether it is comfortable and safe for your playing hand."[26]

This plea to abandon a rigid, didactic approach to pianistic technique in favor of a more natural and individualistic one, has found an active champion of recent years in Dorothy Taubman who directs a School of Music every summer on the campus of Amherst College. Taubman, however, does *not* agree with the Foldes concept of piano-playing as a body-building enterprise. She sees it instead, as a coordinative skill (a development of motion, not muscles), with pain as a clear symbol of incoordination, telling us that something is wrong.[27]

Disciples of the Taubman ideas are increasing across the country, and the author has recently encountered two of them: Jane Abbott-Kirk of Baylor University, in a workshop for piano teachers, and Daniel Epstein of the Raphael Trio, in a seminar and master-class for college-level piano students. Both are eloquent proponents of the principal Taubman concepts: a natural hand position (just as the arm hangs, fingers not artificially curled); the elimination of hand stretching and twisting, and of finger isolation; the use of fingers and arm together with extensive employment of forearm rotation; and the adaptation of fingering and notation to promote the pianist's health and comfort.

This new view of pianistic technique has even gone so far as to solve the problem posed by the Schnabel quotation in the previous section, that of weak fingers on important musical lines. Taubman holds that these fingers are weak only when isolated, and can be as strong as the others when fingers, hand, and arm work as a unit in supporting rotary and lateral motions.

We have then, in the Taubman system, one possible answer to the epidemic of pianists currently being diagnosed by musical medicine as victims of "overuse". It begins to appear as though, in many cases, "misuse" rather than "overuse" may indeed be the initiating cause of certain disabilities. The path to their avoidance may involve not only proper body alignment, as taught in the Alexander Technique, but the best pedagogical guidance in the motion and use of the hands, arms, and fingers as well.

Fortunately, scientists are now beginning to join with pedagogues in studies in these areas. Some of these are chronicled in recent articles such as "Pianists' Hand Ergonomics and Touch Control"[28] and "Minimization of Finger Joint Forces and Tendon Tensions in Pianists"[29]: both describing attempts to determine those uses of the fingers and hand that will help to prevent pianists' pain and injuries. Performers would be well advised to stay current on relevant pedagogical and scientific findings, in the face of increasing evidence that an "ounce of prevention" will serve to avoid the necessity of the psychologically and financially costly "pound of cure".

Cherchez le piano

Most of us have encountered the French phrase "cherchez la femme", often used by speakers or writers to mean "look for the woman" as a causative factor in a given situation. Titling this section "cherchez le piano", then, indicates *this* writer's concern that the very instruments over which we pianists labor may, at least in some cases, be a contributing factor to the "overuse" and "misuse" treated above.

In the spring of 1989, an article by Edward Rothstein in the *New Republic* reviewed the twentieth-century history of the piano in the United States.[30] It is a distressing picture, characterized by a decreasing number of manufacturers, increased emphasis on investment potential, and appalling decline in quality of the instruments because of the gradual disappearance of knowledgeable craftsmen. Along with this decline is the rising incidence of disabling conditions of the hand, even among our finest and most experienced concert pianists, such as Leon Fleischer and Gary Graffman. Reading Graffman's own words describing the history of his problem, a chilling picture begins to emerge.

"Twelve years earlier," he says, "when I played the Tchaikovsky First Concerto with the Berlin Philharmonic, the instrument I had to use was hideously unresponsive. No matter what I did, no sound."[31] He then tells how he began to use the first and third fingers for powerful octave playing when pitted against symphony orchestras. (Note Dorothy Taubman's warning that anything other than the first to the fifth fingers for octaves is a potentially dangerous stretch.)

Eventually, Graffman and his doctors began to draw the connections between his disability and his playing activities. In the process, the science of musical medicine was born, and Graffman continues his crusade by exhorting doctors not to "overlook the simple fact that the constant whomping of a resistant piano key by a tender . . . finger . . . may cause bizarre and remarkable symptoms."[32]

With nightmarish words such as "resistant" and "hideously unresponsive" echoing in our ears, we begin to perceive that the contemporary pianist's relationship to his instrument may gradually be changing from "love" to "war", and that he may, furthermore, be losing the battle. Priscilla and Joel Rappaport, Master Builders who hold diplomas from the Handwerkskammer in Stuttgart, and who have maintained the Van Cliburn competition pianos for almost a decade, believe we are in a crisis situation. In their opinion, actions in the majority of grand pianos built in this country are too heavy and unresponsive, and they feel that this may indeed be a factor in the growing number of hand problems among pianists, and of medical clinics being established to treat them.[33]

The warning hereby sounded is a reminder to aspiring young pianists (and more experienced ones as well) not to pound away incessantly at an unfriendly action, and to assiduously avoid the "no pain, no gain" philosophy of building technique. We should also keep in mind that a coordinated, comfortable use of the body and a responsive instrument are essentials to our art form, and should consider any discomfort to be an early sign of a possibly troublesome course that is in imminent need of correction.

ENDNOTES FOR PART I

1. See Fry, H.J.H. "Overuse syndrome in musicians: prevention and management," *Lancet* 2:728–731, 1986. Fry recommends a five minute break following every twenty-five minutes of practice.

2. Bella Davidovich in Noyle, Linda J. *Pianists on Playing* (Metuchen, NJ: Scarecrow, 1987), p. 43.

3. See Grindea, Carola. "Piano Playing" in *Tensions in the Performance of Music* (New York: Alexander Broude, 1978), pp. 108–109.

4. Bernstein, Seymour. *With Your Own Two Hands* (New York: Schirmer Books, 1981), p. 66–67.

5. See Bibliography below for books by and about F.M. Alexander.

6. The writer would like to acknowledge her work with Alice Dutcher Thornton, certified Alexander instructor and teacher of the Alexander Technique at Incarnate Word College, San Antonio, Texas, as the source of much of the information in this section.

7. Caplan, Deborah. *Back Trouble* (Gainesville, FL: Triad Publishing Co., 1987), p. 18.

8. See photographs of performers' hands in Gat, Jozsef. *The Technique of Piano Playing* (London: Collet's, 1964).

9. See Matthay, Tobias. *The Visible and Invisible in Pianoforte Technique* (London: Oxford University Press, 1932).

10. Hoare, Rodney. "What did Matthay mean?" *Piano Teacher* 4:2–3 n4 1962, p. 3.

11. Op. cit. Alice Thornton: information of preceding two paragraphs.

12. For relevance of the technique to pianists, see:
(a)Altman, Elenore. "Ideas from Yoga about Body Posture and Hand Position," *Clavier* 8:29–31 n2 1969, and
(b)Wolff, Konrad. "Yoga for Pianists," *Clavier* 7:14–19 n7 1968.

13. Gross, Gail. "T'ai Chi Ch'uan in the Art of Practice (Piano Practicing as a Meditative Art Form)," *Piano Quarterly* 38:53–56 n148 1989–90, pp. 55–56.

14. In a recent survey, half of a group of high school musicians were already demonstrating overuse injury: Lockwood, A.H. "Medical problems in secondary school-aged musicians," *Medical Problems of Performing Artists* 3:129–32, 1988.

15. Lockwood, A.H. "Medical problems of musicians," *New England Journal of Medicine* 320:221–27, 1989.

16. Critchley, M. and R. Henson, eds. *Music and the Brain:* studies in the neurology of music (Springfield, IL: Charles C Thomas, 1977).

17. Sataloff, Robert T., Alice G. Brandfonbrenner and Richard J. Lederman. *Textbook of Performing Arts Medicine* (New York: Raven Press, 1991).

18. A selected list of the leading clinics is to be found in the following article: Cockey, Linda et al. "A Teaching Strategy for Healthier Performers," *American Music Teacher* 38:22 + n3 1989.

19. Chleboun, Gary S. and Gail J. Berenson. "Decreased Flexibility of the First Lumbrical: A Case Study," *Medical Problems of Performing Artists* 4:86–90 n2 1989.

20. Rosenthal, Eleanor. "The Alexander Technique: What It Is and How It Works," *American Music Teacher* 39:24–27 + n2 1989, p. 27.

21. Pierce, Alexandra. "Doing and Overdoing in Performance," *Piano Quarterly* 22:40–41 + n87 1974, p. 41.

22. Ibid, p. 40.

23. Pierce, Alexandra and Roger Pierce. "Pain and Healing: for Pianists-Part 3," *Piano Quarterly* 32:45–49 n126 1984, p. 45.

24. Schnabel, Artur. "The Hand and the Keyboard," *Etude* 70:13+ February, 1952, p. 13.

25. Manduca, Liz. "The Athletic Pianist," *Clavier* 24:19–21 n7 1985.

26. Foldes, Andor. "It's All Done with Muscles," *Etude* 69:15+ February, 1951, p. 62.

27. See Rezit, Joseph. "Miracle in Massachusetts: Dorothy Taubman," *Clavier* 27:24–28 n3 1988.

28. Lee, Sang-Hie. "Pianists' Hand Ergonomics and Touch Control," *Medical Problems of Performing Artists* 5:72–78 n2 1990.

29. Harding, David C. et al. "Minimization of Finger Joint Forces and Tendon Tensions in Pianists," *Medical Problems of Performing Artists* 4:103–8 n3 1990.

30. Rothstein, Edward. "Don't Shoot the Piano," *New Republic* 32–35 May 1, 1989.

31. Graffman, Gary."Doctor, can you lend an ear?" *Medical Problems of Performing Artists* 1:3–6 1986, p. 4.

32. Ibid, p. 6.

33. Priscilla and Joel Rappaport operate a piano workshop in Round Rock, Texas. They have both worked extensively in the Bechstein, Boesendorfer, and Steinway factories of Germany and Austria.

BIBLIOGRAPHY FOR PART I

Alexander, F.M. *The Use of the Self* (Long Beach, CA: Centerline Press, 1984).

Explanation of the development and methodology of the Alexander Technique by its originator.

Alexander, F.M. *Constructive Conscious Control of the Individual* (Long Beach, CA: Centerline Press, 1985).

Contains detailed descriptions of procedures used in a typical Alexander lesson. Concepts of "endgaining" and "sensory appreciation" are introduced.

Altman, Elenore. "Ideas from Yoga about Body Posture and Hand Position," *Clavier* 8:29–31 n2 1969.

Exercises to achieve relaxation and balance of body and hand at the piano.

Babits, Linda and Hillary Mayers. "The Path to Productive Practicing," *American Music Teacher* 38:24 + n2 1988.

Using the Alexander Technique to observe body use and identify problems while practicing and memorizing.

Barford, Philip J. "Mind, Hands and Keyboard," *Music and Letters* 36:226–32 n3 1955.

Explication of "Ideo-Kinesis" system in *New Pathways to Piano Technique* (see Bonpensiere, Luigi, below).

Bernstein, Seymour. *With Your Own Two Hands* (New York: Schirmer Books, 1981).

Excellent contemporary treatment of many areas vital to the pianist (practicing, concentration, points of technique, memorizing, breathing, etc.).

Berumen, Ernesto. "High or Close Finger Action?" *Musical Courier* 142:39 n4 1950.

High fingers build strength, close fingers legato and warmth of tone. Both are needed.

Bonpensiere, Luigi. *New Pathways to Piano Technique* (New York: Philosophical Library, 1953).
Description of "Ideo-Kinesis": intense concentration on willing the musical end-result, coupled with complete unconcern about physical movements.

Boyd, Mary Boxall. "Between the Diploma and the Concert Stage," *Musical Courier* 156:6–7 n7 1957.

Schnabel's teaching assistant writes of the need to develop relaxed "body resilience" which enables technical ease and concentrated inner listening.

Brandfonbrenner, Alice G. "The Medical Problems of Musicians," *American Music Teacher* 37:11 + n5 1988.

The director of the Northwestern Medical Program for Performing Artists and editor of the journal *Medical Problems of Performing Artists* surveys some of the most common problems, while discussing therapeutic and preventive strategies.

———. "Preliminary Findings from the MTNA Music Medicine Survey," *American Music Teacher* 39:14–15 + n1 1989.

Unlike the International Conference of Symphony and Opera Musicians survey of orchestral musicians, which indicated an injury frequency of 76 percent, Music Teachers' National Association members show an overall injury rate of only 29 percent.

———. "MTNA Music Medicine Survey Part 2: The Teachers," *American Music Teacher* 39:20–23 + n3 1989.

Report continues with findings on connections of injuries to lifestyle and habits.

Bridges, A.K. "A cognitively oriented concept of piano technique," *Dissertation Abstracts* 47:114 A July, 1986.

Principles of psycho-physiology are coordinated into a unified system of piano technique, which stresses performance goals rather than body movements.

Brower, Harriet. *The Art of the Pianist: Technic and Poetry in Piano Playing* (New York: Carl Fischer, 1911).

Much of the material is dated, but contains an interesting chapter with photographs on "restructuring the hands."

Bryant, Celia Mae. "Keyboard Problems and Physical Solutions," *Clavier* 3:15–17 + n4 1964.

Guidance (with suggested exercises) for solving technical problems of hand, fingers, arm, shoulders.

Caplan, Deborah. *Back Trouble* (Gainesville, FL: Triad Publishing Co., 1987).

A clear, approachable presentation of the Alexander Technique as applied to daily activities, with many useful photographs. Chapter called "The Performing Artist's Dilemma" describes retraining for good body use while practicing.

Chleboun, Gary S. and Gail J. Berenson. "Decreased Flexibility of the First Lumbrical: A Case Study," *Medical Problems of Performing Artists* 4:86–90 n2 1989.

A physical therapist describes successful treatment with mild stretching exercises of a pianist's non-performance-related injury to the right index finger.

Cockey, Linda et al. "A Teaching Strategy for Healthier Performance," *American Music Teacher* 38:22 + n3 1989.

Outlines a teaching stategy for preventing performance-related maladies. Includes a useful list of performing arts medical programs across the country.

Cohen, Leonardo G. and Mark Hallett. "Hand cramps: clinical features and electromyographic patterns in a focal dystonia," *Neurology* 38:1005–12, 1988.

Study of 19 patients with hand cramps includes four pianists whose careers were seriously affected.

Fishbein, Martin and Susan Middlestadt. "Medical Problems Among ICSOM Musicians: Overview of a National Survey," *Medical Problems of Performing Artists* 3:1–8 March, 1988.

Fully 76% of musicians performing with 48 orchestras reported at least one severe medical performance problem: stage fright and pain in the neck and back were most frequently mentioned.

Foldes, Andor. "It's All Done With Muscles," *Etude* 69:15 + February, 1951.

Author does not believe in a fixed hand position or fingering; piano should be fit to the hand.

Fry, H.J.H. "Overuse syndrome in musicians: prevention and management," *Lancet* 2:728–31, 1986.

Techniques for alleviating overuse syndrome include safe practice habits (such as breaks every half hour) and various regimens for resting affected parts.

Gat, Jozsef. *The Technique of Piano Playing* (London: Collet's, 1964).

Details of finger and body use in all types of technical problems. Many useful photographs of pianists' hands on keyboard.

Graffman, Gary. "Doctor, can you lend an ear?," *Medical Problems of Performing Artists* 1:3–6, 1986.

Graffman tells the history of his hand injury and his participation in the growth of the musical medicine specialty.

Grindea, Carola, ed. *Tensions in the Performance of Music* (New York: Alexander Broude, 1978).

A collection of writings which includes excellent articles by Nelly Ben-Or on "The Alexander Technique" and by the editor on the use of the body to minimize tension in "Piano Playing".

Gross, Gail. "T'ai Chi Ch'uan in the Art of Piano Practice," *Piano Quarterly* 38:53–56 n148 1989–90.

The Chinese Taoist exercises of T'ai Chi Ch'uan utilize essential qualities that pianists need to incorporate in their practicing: slowness, lightness, clarity, calmness, and balance.

Harding, David C., Kenneth D. Brandt, and Ben M. Hillberry. "Minimization of Finger Joint Forces and Tendon Tensions in Pianists," *Medical Problems of Performing Artists* 4:103–8 n3 1989.

Study attempts to determine finger positions which will minimize development of musculoskeletal pain and injuries in pianists.

Henson, R.A. and H.Urich. "Schumann's hand injury," *British Medical Journal* 1:900–03, 1978.

Suggests a nerve disorder more likely to have caused Schumann's hand injury, rather than a mechanical device.

Hoare, Rodney. "What did Matthay mean?" *Piano Teacher* 4:2–3 n4 1962.

A student of Matthay's explains some of his frequently used terms that have been wrongly interpreted.

Hochberg, Fred H., Robert D.Leffert et al. "Hand Difficulties Among Musicians," *Journal of the American Medical Association* 249:1869–72, 1983.

Study of hand injuries in seventy-five pianists reveals tendonitis as the most common condition, and fourth and fifth fingers of right hand most often involved.

Hope, Eric. *A Handbook of Piano Playing* (London: Dennis Dobson, 1955).

Some interesting comments on touch, tone color, and the "three phases of playing a note".

Knishkowsky, Barry and Richard J.Lederman. "Instrumental Musicians with Upper Extremity Disorders," *Medical Problems of Performing Artists* 1:85–89 n3 1986.

Most frequent diagnosis was musculo-tendinous overuse syndrome involving forearm, wrist, or hand. Follow-up study showed improvement under various therapies.

Kungle, Dr. Sandra. "Self-Reliance for Rhythm and Tempo: Beyond Metronome Dictates," *American Music Teacher* 37:24 + n3 1988.

Discusses relation of rhythmic awareness to the muscular sense of physical pulse and motion.

Lederman, Richard J. "Occupational Cramp in Instrumental Musicians," *Medical Problems of Performing Artists* 3:45–51, 1988.

Of twenty-one patients studied, eight had to change careers. Treatments, such as drugs, rest, bio-feedback, and changes in technique were largely ineffective.

——— and L.H. Calabrese. "Overuse Syndromes in Instrumentalists," *Medical Problems of Performing Artists* 1:7–11 March, 1986.

Clear and concise review of the five major categories of "overuse" syndrome, causative factors, treatment, and possibilities of prevention.

———. "Performing Arts Medicine," *New England Journal of Medicine* 320:246–48 n4 1989.

From the Cleveland Clinic, the author chronicles the recent development (principally since 1977) of performing arts medicine as a specialty area.

———. "An Overview of Performing Arts Medicine," *American Music Teacher* 40:12–15 + n4 1991.

Historical review of performing arts medicine plus a discussion of the three most common problems of musicians: "overuse" syndrome, compression syndromes, and focal dystonias (occupational cramp).

Lee, Sang-Hie. "Pianists' Hand Ergonomics and Touch Control," *Medical Problems of Performing Artists* 5:72–78 n2 1990.

Study done on scale and arpeggio playing by thirteen advanced pianists. Author concludes that examinations of relationships between size and shape of hand, and movements and functions of the joints may be important to healthy musical training.

Levine, Henry. "Athletes at the Keyboard," *Etude* 68:16 + June, 1950.

Utilization at the keyboard of basic techniques from the world of sports, such as getting into position before striking.

Lockwood, Alan H. "Medical problems in secondary school-aged musicians," *Medical Problems of Performing Artists* 3:129–32 1988.

A study of performance-related disabilities already affecting a number of musicians still in their high-school years.

————. "Medical Problems of Musicians," *New England Journal of Medicine* 320:221–26 n4 1989.

A fine review article by the former head of the Performing Artists Clinic, University of Texas Medical School, Houston. Discusses causes of difficulty and therapeutic approaches. Also includes extensive bibliography.

———— and Mark L. Lindsay. "Reflex sympathetic dystrophy after overuse: the possible relationship to focal dystonia," *Medical Problems of Performing Artists* 4:114–17 n3 1989.

Case studies of three pianists who developed pain and swelling after overuse, of greater intensity than would be expected from the initial problem. The appearance of RSD emphasized the need for better understanding of the pathophysiology of the "overuse" syndrome.

Manchester, Ralph A. "The Incidence of Hand Problems in Music Students," *Medical Problems of Performing Artists* 3:15–18 December, 1988.

At one university music school, 5% to 11% of performance majors developed hand problems each year, during a four year period. Women appeared to be at greater risk than men, and keyboard and string players at greater risk than other instrumentalists.

Manduca, Liz. "The Athletic Pianist," *Clavier* 24:19–21 n7 1985.

Compares piano practicing to athletics, suggesting activities and attitudes for warm-up, "the game" itself, cool-down, and between "games".

Mastroianni, Thomas. "Technique Born Free," *Piano Quarterly* 34:56–59 n134 1986.

Examines bodily distortions that can hamper efficient technique, such as elevated shoulders; high, stiff wrist; overly raised fingers, etc.

Matthay, Tobias. *First Principles of Pianoforte Playing* (London: Bosworth & Co., 1905).

Detailed examination of the muscular components of "touch".

————. *The Visible and Invisible in Pianoforte Technique* (London: Oxford University Press, 1932).

Systematic description of finger, arm, and hand use in this now famous technical approach.

"The Music Clinic," *Lancet* 1:1309–10, 1985.

Hand difficulties of pianists with particular composers' works. Cramp, pain, and weakness mid-career symptoms, with stiffness more prevalent in elderly.

Noyle, Linda J., editor. *Pianists on Playing: Interviews with Twelve Concert Pianists.* (Metuchen, NJ: Scarecrow Press, 1987).

Interviews with twelve pianists ranging in age from Rudolph Firkušný (born 1912) to André-Michel Schub (born 1952), asking the same fifteen questions on the pianist's craft (practicing, memorizing, performing, etc.).

Ortmann, Otto. *The Physiological Mechanics of Piano Technique* (New York: E.P.Dutton and Co., 1962).

Originally published in 1929, this is a comprehensive study on the nature of muscular action as used in piano playing, and the effects of this action upon the piano key and piano tone.

Pierce, Alexandra. "Doing and Overdoing in Performance," *Piano Quarterly* 22:40–41 + n87 1974.

Discussion of unnecessary physical and mental tensions in performance and how to avoid them.

———— and Roger Pierce. "Pain and Healing: for Pianists-Part 2," *Piano Quarterly* 31:38–41 n122 1983.

"Reverberation," the release-through of movement, is preventive and healing to the chronic tension which causes most of the pain in piano playing.

———— and ————. "Pain and Healing: for Pianists-Part 3," *Piano Quarterly* 32:45–49 n126 1984.

Excellent article on proper sitting at the piano. Discusses pelvic support, neck, shoulders, feet, etc.

Rezit, Joseph. "Miracle in Massachusetts: Dorothy Taubman," *Clavier* 27:24–28 n3 1988.

Taubman's approach to technique concentrates on avoiding "mis-use" of hands and fingers.

Robert, Walter. "Fingering," *Clavier* 12:813 n2 1973.

Principles behind fingering of scales, arpeggios, chords, and non-technical passage-work.

Rosenthal, Eleanor. "The Alexander Technique-What It Is and How It Works," *Medical Problems of Performing Artists* 2:53–57 n2 1987.

History and description of the Alexander Technique; its use with three disabled performing musicians.

Rothstein, Edward. "Don't Shoot the Piano," *New Republic* 32–35 May 1, 1989.

Chronicles the decline of twentieth-century piano building in the United States.

Sataloff, Robert T., Alice Brandfonbrenner, and Richard J. Lederman. *Textbook of Performing Arts Medicine* (New York: Raven Press, 1991).

The first published textbook in this new medical specialty, dealing with injuries and occupational hazards to instrumentalists, singers, and dancers.

Schmied, Al. "The Importance of Developing Kinesthetic (Finger) Memory in Piano Performance," *American Music Teacher* 23:11–12 n5 1974.

Practicing difficult passages with closed eyes improves control of spatial formations and skips, and strengthens inner listening.

Schnabel, Artur. "The Hand and the Keyboard," *Etude* 70:13 + February, 1952.

Observes that the hand is not naturally adapted to the keyboard, and suggests ways to compensate.

Stiehl, James B. "Overuse Syndrome in Professional Keyboard Musicians," *American Organist* 23:80–81 n9 1989.

Commonly encountered hand problems of keyboard players: diagnosis, treatment, and prevention.

Taylor, Harold. *The Pianist's Talent* (New York: Taplinger, 1979).

An approach to piano playing based on the remarkable convergence of views held by F.M. Alexander and piano pedagogue, Raymond Thiberge.

Whiteside, Abby. *The Pianist's Mechanism* (New York: G. Schirmer, 1929).

Analysis of the contributions of shoulder, arm, wrist, and thumb to the mechanism of piano playing.

———. *Indispensables of Piano Playing* (New York: Chas. Scribner's, 1955).

A noted teacher shares many of her insights, including the link between the inner hearing and the movements prompted in piano playing.

Wilson, Frank R. "Teaching Hands, Treating Hands," *Piano Quarterly* 36:34–41 n141 1988.

A physician urges teachers, performers, and doctors to participate in research on motor control, so that the causes of focal dystonia (occupational cramp) may be discovered.

Wolff, Konrad. "Yoga for Pianists," *Clavier* 7:14–19 n7 1968.

Suggested Yoga postures to bring about firming, strengthening, and sensitizing of fingers, hands, wrists, and arms; also to promote relaxation and vitality.

Ziporyn, Terra. "Pianist's cramp to stage fright: the medical side of music-making," *Journal of the American Medical Association* 252:985–89 n8 1984.

Describes a number of physical and psychological problems of musicians, and some of the conferences and clinics now being set up to deal with them.

PART II   MIND

MOTIVATION

Despite an immense literature on the subject, controversy continues to rage concerning the exact location and constitution of "the mind". Fortunately for our purposes, we do not need to trace its physiological and psychological origins, as our principal interest here lies in its functioning: initially, in the capacity of decision making, and subsequently, in the intellectual tasks attendant on implementing these decisions.

For the pianist, the first major category of decision making is one which encompasses all the complexities of motivation behind entering music as a profession. Recent developments in brain research, principally by Howard Gardner, suggest that musical intelligence is one of seven basic modalities of mental functioning and therefore universally available for development.[1] Commenting on this work, which he sees as conferring a "biological guarantee of musicianship," Donald Hodges finds it leading to still another important concept:

> Musical intelligence, he says, provides us with a way of knowing about the world and our relationship to it that is no better, no worse than any other type of intelligence. Just as a person would be impoverished if he lacked an education in language or mathematics, so is he impoverished if he lacks a musical education. Music provides valuable insights into the human condition that are unique, and that cannot be gained through other means.[2]

This, certainly, is good news to the music teachers of the world. It is also good news to all those who care about the uses of mankind's increasing leisure in pursuit of artistic, cultural,

Figure 2. " Teachers will perceive that a pianist is in the making."

and even spiritual growth. If piano playing, then, is potentially available to all, what is it that draws a few of us to cross the line between a life-enriching hobby and a life-dominating obsession?

First and most obvious, of course, is the discovery of talent beyond the ordinary. If the hand adapts naturally to the keyboard, the reading skills develop speedily, and all seem joined to serve a sensitive musical instinct, teachers and

Figure 3. " A humble medium between the composers and audiences of the world."

parents will perceive that a pianist is in the making. The talented child or adolescent will then receive considerable reinforcement in the form of praise and perhaps competitive success from his surroundings. But by the time he is in high-school and faced with the imminent choosing of a life's work, hard questions will have to be addressed: "Is my talent sufficient to enable me to earn a living in music?"; "Do I want to be a performer, a teacher, or a combination of the two?"; and last, but by no means least, "Am I suited for a career in music?"

Motivation is the key that will unlock the answer to the third and most difficult question. It must be recognized that a career in music requires extraordinary discipline, devotion, and grueling work, as well as the capacity for delayed gratification, all of which are becoming uncommon in our push-button world. Add to this the unlikelihood of impressive monetary reward, and one might well conclude, as has the writer, that the only good reason for becoming a pianist is the presence of such an all-consuming desire that one cannot bring oneself to do anything else.

Even then, the last word has not been spoken. For this desire, even in the highly talented, must not be merely a vision of fame, glory, and affluence, or it will not survive the exigencies of competition, critics, performance anxiety, all-weather travel, and lonely hotel rooms. Only an overwhelming love of music and a strongly felt need to become a humble medium between the composers and the audiences of the world are sufficient goads to spending one's life in the service of this art form. In the long haul, nothing lesser will sustain us.

ORGANIZATION

When approached from the point of view of organization and control, the study of the piano can serve as an arresting metaphor for Life. The author has often had in the studio the experience of watching an initially confused and unassertive student grow in confidence, clarity, and initiative as he gains mastery over the organization of his daily schedule and learning habits.

Practice-Scheduling

Careful scheduling is certainly important to any busy student, but to the musician it is an almost desperate necessity. Juggling all the obvious demands of classes, papers, and examinations with the part-time jobs which today's tuitions make almost mandatory, he must still find time to practice his instrument. And he must do it without having to forego sleep, nourishment, and occasional restorative periods of leisure. Nowadays, there is no way to accomplish this without a detailed schedule which explicitly designates daily practice time:-always the first item to evaporate from an unplanned agenda. Nor does this problem disappear when student days are left behind. Unless one is working as a paid performer, in which case preparing the music automatically serves this function, practice time must be jealously guarded. Teachers are particularly prone to serve their students first, and their own performing skills last, which inevitably leads to the atrophy of those skills with the passage of time. The pianist-teacher's creed must be to make regular performance opportunities and personal practice time absolute priorities, if he is to maintain the joyful experience of high-level music-making and thereby be an example to his students.

Many pianists find their optimum practice time to be first thing in the morning, while those with other bio-rhythms, who barely stumble out of bed, prefer a somewhat later session. It is universally true, however, that to save practice time for the tired end of a long, busy day, is to ensure little accomplishment, since the careful, concentrated listening so essential to meaningful results will then be difficult to achieve. Admittedly, it is better to move the fingers on the keyboard without the brain's participation than not to move them at all, but the diminution in the quality of learning in a state of mental fatigue must be recognized. The pianist Misha Dichter puts it this way:

> In practicing, never daydream. Never use the piano as a vehicle for simply moving the fingers and passing time. If you have only one moment when you're not aware of what you're doing musically or technically (and usually both), you're wasting your time.[3]

Practice-Methodology

Having seated himself at the piano, the serious pianist must now exert intellectual control to make the most of his precious available time. If he applies the principles of analytical practicing, he will minimize the period of dry, technical learning, and arrive with the greatest speed at the point of musical mastery.

The basic key to analytical practicing is the concept of taking things apart into small, manageable sections. The first item to be thus dissected is the practice period itself. A workable scheme is to allow one segment for a warm-up period of scales and exercises, a segment for each work of the literature being studied, and at least five to ten minutes for sight-reading of new material. This sight-reading period can occur directly after the warm-up, between pieces, or at the end of the session, but should always be included, as it is one of the most important parts of the pianist's technical and musical development.

Complementing this initial division of time, is the next step of dividing each work to be studied into sections that can be successfully addressed in each day's practice. A single "read-through" of the entire composition before beginning its study is recommended, so as to gain an initial sense of the whole. Thereafter, the detailed work of learning notes, rhythms, phrasing, and fingering should be carefully undertaken, and reading-through for the most part avoided until the final section has been digested.

The allotted time for each section may be spent on such familiar tasks as hands alone and together practicing in short phrases, assigning fingerings, addressing difficult leaps and passage-work, and stabilizing rhythm with a metronome. Samuel Viviano reminds us, however, that working with a metronome cannot be allowed to be too protracted or mechanical, but must be a conscious process aimed at the development of a dependable inner pulse. Conducting the passage with the metronome, playing from slower to progressively faster speeds, and constantly stopping to evaluate one's performance are all part of this process. Closely allied is the development of the ability to feel specific tempo markings with the inner hearing, which necessitates a routine of working alternately with and without the metronome.[4]

To be avoided, also, is mindless repetition of playing errors, in the hope that they will be magically corrected. Analytical practicing, at its most effective in this situation, requires that the *reason* for the error be uncovered by a series of questions: "Is the fingering awkward?"; "Does the hand position need to be adjusted?"; "Is the eye or hand taking too long to travel to the next required location?"; "Is tension in any part of the arm or hand inhibiting movement?"; and so on. Once the answer is established, the problem can be dealt with and conquered in far less time than is required by the "repeat and pray" method.

Modern technology has also made it possible for us to analyze our practicing *aurally* by recording our playing and subjecting it to our own critical ears. Difficult as it is initially to listen to oneself perform, it is a habit worth cultivating, as it yields enormous dividends of insight into needed areas of work in technique and musicianship.[5]

Memorizing

Educational psychologists have identified at least four major learning modes that are involved in memorizing a piece of music:

1. Aural-what it sounds like
2. Tactile-what it feels like
3. Visual-what it looks like (both score and keyboard)
4. Theoretical-its harmonic and motivic structure

Interestingly, individuals have varying degrees of endowment in these four areas, and almost everyone finds it necessary to deliberately cultivate one or more for purposes of increased security and control.

"Aural" (treated at greater length below) and "tactile" are perhaps the most intuitive, or we might say "right-brain," members of this foursome:-the ones that seem to come with least effort, but can be, for some people, most evanescent and least dependable. They usually need to be reinforced by the more linear components of the actual appearance of the notes on the page and, especially, the theoretical analysis of how the formal elements of key, harmony, melody, and texture have been put together by the composer.

During the past several decades, many excellent "methods" of piano study have advocated memorizing a piece of music from back to front, so that one now finds numerous players committed to this approach. It seems to embody some psychologically sound principles, and is especially recommended for players who have a tendency to memorize the beginnings of works with alacrity, and the conclusions with great difficulty or not at all. Rebecca Shockley, a staunch advocate of this method, explains why, in her opinion, it is effective:

> One important reason is that it tends to reduce our dependence on what psychologists refer to as 'serial memory' in which a series of items can be remembered only in succession. . . . Practicing [and memorizing] 'backwards' helps to increase awareness of each part—as a potential starting point and in relation to the whole—so that security is increased.[6]

This writer has found the "backward approach" to memorizing to be favored by many singers in the vocal coaching studio as well as piano students. Regardless of whether the memorizing is begun at the end or the beginning, however, working in sections, with many designated "memory stops" where playing can commence, is strongly advised.

A commonly encountered complaint among pianists playing from memory is visual distraction which prevents concentration, and the author has two suggestions which have proved useful in dealing with this situation. The first is to set up a strong visual focus of one's own choosing, directed at either the choreography of the hands on the keyboard, or the imagined appearance of the notes of the score as seen by the inner eye. The second is to reinforce this focus by the image of a pair of blinders, like those worn by street horses, surrounding one's eyes and cutting off any sights or events other than score or keyboard.

All pianists should work to underline the above processes with a firm aural control of the music prompted by inner hearing, which means continuously imagining the sound of the music just before it is played. Larson and Van Auken stress that "training the student's inner hearing is as important as training their minds to react accurately and to read notation. Ultimately," they insist, "inner hearing should lead the muscles", not vice-versa, and "students should not only practice playing a piece, they should practice imagining a piece."[7]

Yet another aspect of memorizing brings us back to the Alexander Technique, and concepts involving "good use" of the total body in the performer's habitual learning activities. The warning sounded here is that memorizing should not be done in a state of bodily tension, because the brain and nervous system will record the tension along with the notes, resulting in an imprint for anxious performance. The process to be avoided is described by Alexander teachers Linda Babits and Hilary Myers in these terms:

> If one is silently memorizing a piece of music and sitting in such a way that his postural muscles cannot support him appropriately, then other muscles—most likely the shoulders and neck—will be doing the job, producing strain and stress and probably causing contractions of the arms into the back. This, then, will be memorized along with the music. . . . This, of course, holds true for learning new pieces as well.[8]

It is clear that memorizing, like all practice activities, should take place in a relaxed, alert, well-rested consciousness for maximal results.

One final, meaningful note on memorizing is sounded by Bela Nagy in a *Clavier* article written twenty-five years ago but still highly pertinent to the subject. Says Nagy:

> A quite unnatural and unnecessary emphasis has been placed on playing by memory. . . . The fact that somebody plays something from memory has not much to do with the value of his interpretation. You can interpret something at an extremely high level from the score, and you can misinterpret something without the score.[9 a,b]

He goes on to point out great pianists such as Bartok and Dame Myra Hess who rarely played from memory, and to advocate deciding early on in the school year which pieces will be memorized when the curriculum demands this. The idea behind the latter procedure, and one in which this writer heartily concurs, is to leave time for studying the vast reaches of the piano literature more extensively. Few of us could argue that the currently widespread university level piano requirement of three memorized pieces for end-of-the-semester "juries" and a memorized graduation recital leaves all too little room to fill in the large repertoire gaps with which students frequently begin their college work. Memorizing, in short, should not dominate the process of pianistic learning and development, but should serve it.

Sight-Reading

As will be pointed out in the section on Long Range Planning, certain types of pianistic careers necessitate a particularly high-level development of sight-reading ability. It is also true, however, that *all* professional pianists need to cultivate this skill assiduously, as it is crucial both in the rapid learning of new performance material and as the tool which enables widely ranging acquaintance with all the many varieties of keyboard literature.

William S. Newman, in his comments on "Sight-Reading for Profit and Pleasure" advises the developing pianist to work through whole volumes of the standard literature,

> "choosing according to the limits of his technique and musical understanding, transferring from one era and style to another for variety and a balanced diet, and keeping a dated record of what he plays. . . . If he is studying a Mozart sonata, a Chopin prelude, or any other piece that is one among many of its kind, he can extend his general perspective and his understanding of that piece by reading all of its fellows in the same volume."[10]

He goes on to advise writing brief but careful comments in a sight-reading notebook, which will serve as a guide for future repertoire decisions.

With the necessity, then, for good pianistic sight-reading skills being clearly drawn, what help is there for a performer who has a fine musical ear and good technical equipment but whose reading speed remains unacceptably slow? Music reading, in this writer's experience, is very akin to word reading, with the added component of kinesthetic (bodily) response added on to symbol translation. Rapid word readers tend to read music rapidly and vice versa. Of recent years, studies in patterns of eye movements aimed at improving word reading speed have also suggested concepts which are adaptable to the problems of sight-reading at the piano.

It is now generally recognized that the visual techniques of successful sight-reading require: taking in as much notation as possible at each glance; constantly looking ahead to the next measure or staff; and keeping one's gaze fixed on the score while seeing the keyboard peripherally (or by quickly lowering the eyes without dropping the head). Many pedagogues have now begun to consider training in the visual components of sight-reading so important that, like Martha R. Lewis, they are advocating starting reading-ahead training at the very first lesson.

> "Begin by pointing to each note," she says, "[and then] by moving the the pencil point across the blank area of the staff between one note and the next. The student will instinctively follow the pointer, moving his eyes to the upcoming note,"[11] *and a sight-reader has been born.* (Author's words in italics)

Many texts on sight-reading have been published for the purpose of building these skills in the intermediate and even advanced pianist. One of the best, which has only recently appeared on the market, is *Keyboard Sight-Reading* by Ellen Baumeister,[12] a text specifically aimed at the college level keyboard player who has difficulty sight-reading. In this book, Ms. Baumeister offers a well-formulated presentation of the major elements of sight-reading ability, together with many musically interesting exercises and new, imaginative views of old problems.

Chapter headings such as "Soft Eyes," "Eyes in Motion," and "Peripheral and Agile Vision" are graphically suggestive of the needed physical responses, while sections on score-reading, horizontal intervals, vertical reading, and fingerings that maintain key contact successively address individual aspects of the overall problem. Baumeister's unique opening section on "Flexibility" upholds the thesis that good sight-readers should be able to read even in the face of simultaneous distraction, and exercises are undertaken to promote the ability to play while holding a conversation, while standing up, etc.

Sight-reading, then, has finally come into its own. No longer considered a mysterious gift, bestowed by the universe on a few lucky pianists, and ignored by the unlucky, it has become an area of competence to be cultivated early on and throughout the pianist's career. Few would deny that it is well worth cultivating, as it is the key that unlocks for us all the musical treasures lying in store.

BECOMING A MUSICIAN

Musical Style

At the same time that the emergent pianist is developing skills of practicing, memorizing, and organization, he must also be exercising his intellectual faculties in the cultivation of a sense of musical style. Unfortunately, the notes and other signals on a page of score are only the bare bones of what a pianist worthy of the name of a musician must recognize and recreate. If these are to be fleshed out with appropriate timbre, tempi, phrasing, rhythmic elements, and textural construct, the inner ear must be gradually trained toward a highly sophisticated level of stylistic understanding.

There are a number of avenues leading to this goal. One of the most important is to establish a habit of listening to serious music as early in life as possible. The major benefit of this is that, in the child and adolescent, musical style will be absorbed effortlessly and intuitively, because of the great aural capacities of the young brain:-the same faculty which enables facile language development in childhood.

Parents and teachers can be of assistance here, through the presence of recordings, selection of pertinent radio and TV broadcasts, and giving of appropriate gifts. Not to be overlooked as perhaps the most vital area of the listening habit, is the experience of concert-going, for the sight and sound of fine music in the act of being played has frequently proved the initial spur to many a concert artist's career.

Nor is it necessary, or even desirable, for the pianist to limit himself to concerts of keyboard music. On the contrary, symphony, chamber music, organ, vocal literature, should all be grist to his mill, as he builds familiarity with periods and genres, and begins to explore his own affinities. The difficulty, however, which the writer has encountered in attempting to inculcate this habit in even the most talented students is that, especially during the teen years when peer pressure runs highest, there is reluctance to engage in an activity not sanctioned by the group. School sponsored concerts constitute one method of counteracting this obstacle, and families attending concerts together is another. Needless to say, those who promote and manage concerts need to be keenly aware of the necessity of attracting young concert-goers, since they are the audiences of the future.

The corollary of self-directed listening in the pursuit of musico-stylistic understanding is submitting oneself to an organized course of study. The serious pianist may have encountered limited opportunities for course work in music literature and history in high school, but will most likely begin this on a college level. At this point, many choices must be made, beginning with the type of institution desired (conservatory, liberal arts college, or large university music department) and continuing with the degree program to be undertaken. The Bachelor of Music, with its heavy concentration of performance credits, is probably appropriate only to those having the strongest promise for performing careers, as it is of little use by itself on the musical job market.[13] Music education degrees make the candidate more employable, but traditionally have a somewhat diluted performance emphasis with "methods" courses and elementary work in other instruments.[14] A third option, which is a Bachelor of Arts degree with a music major, deletes performance emphasis, but may still afford considerable opportunity for private instrumental instruction, as well as for the forging of a sensitive musical interpreter through increased study of languages and literature.

Individual strengths, personalities, and goals must be weighed in the selection of an institution and a degree program, but all of them will offer organized course work in the historical development of musical style. Now it becomes more important than ever to apply the new, structured learning with open ears in the concert hall. Student recitals, faculty recitals, visiting artist recitals (again, all media) become the laboratory where critical faculties are honed, and more repertoire than can be played is experienced in the context of period and performance practice.

Pianists must remember that the goal of their hours and years of listening is to develop a secure inner stylistic sound image of all the music they will be playing. Glenn Gould, one of the greatest pianists of the twentieth century, was very emphatic in his remarks on the greater importance of the inner musical idea over repetitive practice:

> One does not play the piano with one's fingers," he said, "one plays the piano with one's mind. If you have a clear image of what you want to do, there's no reason it should . . . need reinforcement. If you don't, all the fine Czerny studies and Hanson exercises in the world aren't going to help you.[15]

Most of us lesser mortals, not gifted by the Gods with Gould's unearthly technical gifts, might not agree to abandon our Hanson and Czerny. We would, however, do well to pay homage, throughout our careers, to the primacy of the musical idea.

Theory

During these same years of study toward mastery of style, the
pianist must also be diligently employing his intellect in the
discipline of music theory. His need for competence in the
areas of harmony, counterpoint, and analysis is fundamental,
both for detailed understanding and recognition of stylistic
components, and for the security that only the structural focus
can bring to the memorizing process.

To be adequately memorized, a work should have under-
gone thorough harmonic analysis of chords and key changes,
motivic and textural analysis of melodic relationships, and
formal analysis of the overall structure. Years of devoted
effort are clearly necessary to acquire these skills, and
fortunately, many methods of piano instruction are now
introducing theoretical work, including transposition and
improvisation, from the earliest stages. Some high schools
also offer theory electives, all of which preparation is highly
recommended. The more background brought to college
level theory, the more sophisticated the pianist's level of
study can be, and the more such upper–level offerings as
orchestration and composition can be entered into with
rewardingly creative results.

LONG-RANGE PLANNING

To Teach or Not to Teach

Following close on the heels of the pianist's initial commitment to a professional career, appears the necessity for a number of smaller but equally crucial decisions. Unless one is certain that a college-level major in piano pedagogy followed by a teaching studio is the desired path, the question of whether or not to teach the instrument *can* be postponed for a period. There are many pianists (the author among them) who, in their years of most intensive training, have been maximally focused on performing and minimally, if at all, interested in teaching. Often, thereafter, teaching opportunities, based on demonstrated mastery of the instrument, will appear. And it is at this point that the performer, finding meaning now in communicating his art–form, will go on to combine his playing with a complementary and satisfying teaching career.

The Soloist

Another choice which will arise as the pianist becomes able to perform on an increasingly mature level, is whether he wants to spend his pianistic life playing as a soloist, or as part of a number of ensemble possibilities (such as symphony member, chamber player, and vocal or choral accompanist).

This choice will be influenced by many personality factors which will in turn determine the level of technical development achieved and the attraction to specific musical genres. A single-minded, highly independent, and assertive student of strong talent may well be drawn to making his own unencumbered musical statements through the solo literature, and to assuming the "star" status of soloist in the concerto with orchestra. The path for this pianist, then, is simple to chart, but is not an easy one. It consists of finding the finest available teachers in the home area (or at a reasonable distance) through middle and high school; auditioning for and enrolling in one of the leading conservatories or strong performing university music departments; then devoting the major portion of daily hours to perfecting the solo repertoire so as to carry it into the competitions which currently showcase young players (see "Recitals and Competitions," p. 93).

Professor of Piano

It must, of course, be recognized that not all players preparing for a soloist's career will make it into the coveted echelon at the top, and be able to sustain themselves solely as traveling concert artists. Many fine young pianists elect to take teaching positions in colleges and universities, whose faculties are particularly eager to add the luster of competition winners to their ranks. This can be a rewarding life, especially if some talented students are available, and can include as much concertizing, both within the institution, and outside it for touring engagements, as the instructor is willing to undertake.

A caveat must be raised here concerning the current climate of opinion in academia regarding the performer, which, especially in liberal arts colleges, often tends to offer him term appointments only, rather than the tenure-track status available to his colleagues teaching music history or theory.

Figure 4. " The 'star' status in the concerto with orchestra."

Bryn Mawr College is one of these, and its president, Pat McPherson, explains that "Bryn Mawr has chosen to follow the Princeton model, the premise of which is that faculty artists are encouraged to keep in touch with their artistic communities and continue their own personal engagements in order not to grow 'stale' in the confines of a small college with a 'captive audience'."[16]

This notion, that the performer should only be removed from the musical mainstream and marketplace for short periods of time, lest his artistry decay from lack of stimulation, is highly debatable at best. Furthermore, its effect is to make second-class citizens of performers even within the music departments themselves. The bright side of the situation is that many performing pianists would indeed prefer the kind of limited commitment to academe that is represented by a "lectureship" or preferably an "artist-in-residence" type of appointment. For those wishing to stay in university teaching, the acquisition of a performing degree at the doctoral level (Doctor of Musical Arts) is strongly recommended as the most certain entrée to the desired privileges of rank and tenure.

Symphony and Chamber Player

A pianist who enjoys ensemble work and is instrumentally oriented, might do well to consider auditioning for the position of keyboard artist with one of the many symphony orchestras in this country. Some of these, it is true, are part-time jobs, but many of the larger orchestras, which may have complicated seasons that include a classical, pops, and educational series, find it advantageous to employ a full-time pianist. In this situation, the performer needs not only a strong technique to be able to negotiate the solo passages of works such as *Petrouchka, Pines of Rome,* etc., but excellent sight-reading skills as well, since preparation time will frequently be very short.

The orchestral keyboard player also needs to be flexible enough to deal with other keyboards besides the piano. Celesta parts occur frequently in orchestral music after 1896 (the year that Tchaikovsky invented the instrument for his "Sugar-Plum Fairy") and Baroque scores will frequently include harpsichord continuo parts. If the symphony plays as an opera orchestra, the so-called dry recitative sections in Mozart and Rossini operas will also require harpsichord continuo. Usually this assignment falls to the orchestral pianist, and it should be noted that, at its artistic best, this is a far more complex skill than even most musicians realize. It requires thorough familiarity with the text and the emotional climate of the dialogue.

The majority of orchestras will have an organist on their roster, if only part-time, but the pianist may be called upon on occasion to play an electric piano or other electronic instrument that does not involve a pedal board. When programming needs demand that the pianist engage in jazz improvisation, however, symphonies will usually hire a player from the outside, unless the keyboard artist has this style in his repertoire.

At times, the symphony pianist may be offered the opportunity to perform as a soloist in a concerto with the orchestra, or in a two-piano solo situation such as the ever-popular *Carnival of the Animals*. Still another advantage of the post is that the orchestra pianist is in the best position to meet and play chamber music with all the finest string and wind players in the area.

Sometimes, a duo or trio situation that begins as peripheral to the orchestra work, may in time become more and more central. It is also possible that a pianist may be called upon frequently to join an established string quartet for performance of piano quartets and quintets. The pianist should then be aware that, for the most part, fees for performing chamber groups are not large, expenses are likely to be high, and it is probably wisest to plan to play this rewarding literature in conjunction with an orchestral or teaching job.

A large part of the challenge and excitement of playing chamber music will be found in the unique demands it makes on the pianist. Unlike the soloist's situation, the chamber player must be constantly aware of the other parts from the standpoints of rhythm, dynamic balance, and motivic contribution to the overall structure. And, equally unlike the

Figure 5. " The challenge and excitement of playing chamber music."

orchestral stance, each player, a conductor being absent, must decide for himself and then negotiate with his fellow players all musical decisions of tempo and interpretation.

Much of the keyboard chamber music, especially from the nineteenth century, is difficult, so a strong technique is needed. Facile sight-reading is again a help, as the pianist always has the most notes to learn, and the ability to read a large portion of the other players' parts while performing one's own is almost mandatory, since only the pianist is in posession of the full score. This also places the major responsibility on the pianist for correcting the ensemble. The ideal personality for a keyboard chamber player therefore becomes one which can suggest rather than assert, and which blossoms under the musical give and take of a group effort toward an artistic goal.

Accompanist/Vocal Coach

The word "accompanist" is incorrectly applied to a pianist who is playing sonatas, trios, or other major works of the instrumental ensemble literature:-the correct term here is "chamber player". If, however, a string or wind player is clearly functioning as soloist (in a concerto reduction, set of Kreisler pieces, etc.), the word "accompanist" is more appropriate since the connotation is that of secondary musical importance, although not necessarily inferior technical demands.

A more widespread use of this term, and one which is always generically correct, involves the whole domain of vocal music, a performance area which the accompanists of the world can rightfully claim could scarcely exist without them. The young pianist being drawn toward this world will find himself using his increasing facility at sight-reading (an indispensable tool for the work) to delve into the vocal literature of art—song and opera. He may well be called upon in high-school and college years to serve as accompanist to glee clubs and choral groups of all kinds, as well as to play for solo singers in contests and performances.

Often, the accompanying proclivity will develop in a player whose literary bent is strong, and who becomes as enamored in his youth of poetry, novels, and drama as he is of sonatas and symphonies. To this pianist, the heightening of words through musical setting will be a constant source of excitement, and he may study voice for a time (whether or not he possesses a performing instrument) in order to be able to understand the singer's perspective, and to exercise his growing empathy with the singer's art.

The pianist who comes to realize that accompanying is his forte is actually in a somewhat more favorable position vis-à-vis employment possibilities than the one bent on a soloist's career. Whereas there are relatively few performing opportunities for soloists, the demand for able accompanists to play with choruses, singers, instrumentalists, opera companies, and dance studios, is much greater, and the accompanist, like the soloist, can always combine his performing with as much teaching as he desires.

What, then, is the course of training for this accompanying-oriented keyboard player? During the past 15 years, many graduate level programs have been established around the country to train accompanists, and a few schools have now begun to offer undergraduate concentrations as well. Whatever the degree program decided upon, the first recommendation is that the player devote as long a time as possible, certainly through the undergraduate years, to continued study of the solo repertoire. This is because the second basic requirement for a fine accompanist (after strong sight-reading) is a universal understanding of musical style, which can best be communicated to the fingers by a thorough grounding in all periods of the solo literature.

All the other methods of cultivating musical style listed above (in course-work, concert-going, and by listening to recorded music) are equally applicable to the accompanist, who, in his listening, will also many times gain the opportunity to critically observe other accompanists at work. Gerald Moore, probably the best known accompanist of the mid-twentieth-century and a strong advocate of the art he practiced, reminds us in *The Unashamed Accompanist* that the pianist's tone quality must also be cultivated to serve the varied stylistic demands of the literature.

> To make his tone blend with a singer or violinist," says Moore, "it is incumbent upon the accompanist . . . to learn to listen to himself. . . . and. . . . to use his fingers with sensitivity and variety of touch. . . . Imagine," he continues, "that a portion of your brain is in each fingertip and eventually you will get a touch sensation according to the variety of tone you want to produce.[17]

Besides all this, verbal and literary skills need to be expanded, which means that courses in literature, theater, and foreign languages should be undertaken to as great an extent as possible in the schedule of a busy music student. A prime reason for the verbal emphasis is that the majority of accompanists in time begin to serve as "coaches" to the singers they accompany:-a complex teaching role which involves helping the vocalist with not only all musical aspects of the repertoire (notes, rhythm, phrasing, etc.) but with details of language and poetic interpretation, as well. Clearly, then, a working knowledge of vocal diction in at least Italian, German, French, and English becomes mandatory for an aspiring coach. The writer has found a knowledge of Spanish and Hebrew to be useful in the studio, as well, and has had occasion to wish for Russian, Czech, and Hungarian.

Kurt Adler, in his exhaustive study of *The Art of Accompanying and Coaching* goes even further in his recommendations for language training. "The accompanist and coach with aspirations," he says, "must know one Romance language well enough to be able to converse fluently, in addition to thoroughly understanding its phonetical, grammatical, and stylistic intricacies."[18] He also considers essential, as does this writer, training in the use of the International Phonetic

Alphabet (IPA) which has a specific sign for every sound, regardless of language of origin.

Besides their many teaching functions, another area in which coaches are frequently called upon for assistance is that of program building. The advice of an experienced coach can be invaluable to singers at all levels, in regard to length of program, selection and grouping of repertoire, key and mood contrast, etc. Clearly, then, the more a pianist can learn of the vocal repertoire, and its appropriateness to different types of voices, the more skill he can offer in this interesting aspect of the coach's expertise.

The accompanist whose prime literary focus is the intimate poetic form will probably specialize in German "lieder" and art-songs of other languages in his coaching and concertizing. The more dramatically oriented pianist may be gradually drawn to playing as a "répétieur" (rehearsal pianist) for opera companies. This may be followed by European travel and work in the opera houses of Italy and Germany, with the eventual goal of becoming an opera coach or perhaps, in time, an assistant or even principal conductor. Many music directors of large opera companies (James Levine, Lawrence Leighton Smith, etc.) have begun as fine pianists working with singers, and have, indeed, never fully abandoned that role.

The vocal accompanist's personality needs to be a felicitous blending of strength and nurturing. Singers tend to be highly-strung, and usually in need of psychological as well as musical support at concert time, so the well-prepared accompanist has the opportunity to ignore or even forsake his own anxiety in the course of reassuring his partner. Needless to say, the accompanist must possess an ego structure that is willing to be submerged, since his ever-present goal is to play a recital so perfectly that he will be virtually unnoticed by all except the most discerning listeners.[19]

Figure 6. " Accompanists are both born and made."

The task of the pianistic chamber-player, as delineated above, is to be a strong, supple, equal partner to his fellow instrumentalists. The vocal accompanist's work is somewhat different. At times he must lead, at times follow, and at times be completely intertwined with the singer. Both intuition and experience will guide him through these choices. Accompanists are both born and made.

ENDNOTES FOR PART II

1. See Gardner, Howard. *Frames of Mind* (New York: Basic Books, 1983).

2. Hodges, Donald A. "Ten Teaching Tips Based on Brain Research," *Texas Music Teacher* 16+ n3 1989, p. 16.

3. Misha Dichter in Noyle, Linda J. *Pianists on Playing* (Metuchen, NJ: Scarecrow Press, 1987), p. 47.

4. See Viviano, Samuel. "The Metronome, its Use and Misuse," *American Music Teacher* 37:28 n1 1987.

5. See Wagner, Jeffrey and Corey Kaup. "Record Yourself at the Piano," *Clavier* 28:17–20 n7 1989.

6. Shockley, Rebecca. "A Backward Approach to Learning Music," *American Music Teacher* 36:32–33 n4 1987, p. 32.

7. Van Auken, Richard and Paul Larson. "Teaching Inner Hearing," *American Music Teacher* 37:17+ n5 1988, pp. 17–18.

8. Babits, Linda and Hillary Mayers. "The Path to Productive Practicing," *American Music Teacher* 38:24+ n2 1988, p. 26.

9.a Nagy, Bela. "Must It Be Memorized?", *Clavier* 4:20–23 n1 1965, p. 21.

9.b Tommasini, Anthony. "Knowing the Score," *Piano Quarterly* 36:48–53 n142 1988. This author describes a shift away from compulsory memorization of concert music by present-day pianists.

10. Newman, William S. *The Pianist's Problems* (New York: Harper and Row, 1974), p. 20.

11. Lewis, Martha R. "How to Teach Sight-Reading," *Clavier* 28:31–32 n7 1989, p. 31.

12. Baumeister, Ellen. *Keyboard Sight-Reading* (Mountain View, CA: Mayfield Publishing Co., 1991).

13. See Rogers, George. "The Bachelor of Music Degree and the Marketplace," *College Music Symposium* 28:106–16, 1988.

14. The most recent trend is toward requiring performance credits in teacher-training programs to be almost equal to those of the Bachelor of Music degree.

15. Glenn Gould in Dubal, David. *Reflections from the Keyboard* (New York: Summit Books, 1984), p. 183.

16. *Bryn Mawr Alumnae Bulletin,* Winter 1989, p. 4.

17. Moore, Gerald. *The Unashamed Accompanist* (London: Methuen and Co., 1959), pp. 24–25.

18. Adler, Kurt. *The Art of Accompanying and Coaching* (Minneapolis: The University of Minnesota Press, 1965), pp. 43–44.

19. See Moore, Gerald. *Am I Too Loud?* (New York: Macmillan, 1962) for insights into the life of an accompanist.

BIBLIOGRAPHY FOR PART II

Adler, Kurt. *The Art of Accompanying and Coaching* (Minneapolis: The University of Minnesota Press, 1965).

History and art of accompanying and coaching; program building; and detailed treatments of Italian, French, German, and Spanish diction.

Arrau, Connie. "Where Are the Jobs? A Look at a Changing Marketplace," *Clavier* 24:52–53 n8 1985.

A study of college-level vacancy listings for pianists, including duties, qualifications, rank offered, and conditions of employment.

Asner, Marie A. "Accompanist and Vocalist: Partners in Music," *American Music Teacher* 37:20–21 n5 1988.

Guidelines for skills, points of etiquette, and personal qualities a singer and accompanist should expect of each other.

Babits, Linda and Hillary Mayers, "The Path to Productive Practicing," *American Music Teacher* 38:24 + n2 1988.

Using the Alexander Technique to observe body use and identify problems while practicing and memorizing.

Banowetz, Joseph. *The Pianist's Guide to Pedaling* (Bloomington: Indiana University Press, 1985).

History of the pedals, discussion of pedaling techniques, and use of the pedal in the major piano repertoire.

Baumeister, Ellen. *Keyboard Sight-Reading* (Mountain View, CA: Mayfield Publishing Co., 1991).

Excellent text-book with many useful exercises for developing sight-reading in the college-level pianist.

Bernstein, Seymour. *With Your Own Two Hands* (New York: Schirmer Books, 1981).

Insightful contemporary treatment of many areas vital to the pianist (practicing, concentration, points of technique, memorizing, breathing, etc.).

Bonpensiere, Luigi. *New Pathways to Piano Technique* (New York: Philosophical Library, 1953).

Description of "Ideo-Kinesis": intense concentration on willing the musical end-result, coupled with complete unconcern about physical movements.

Bridges, A.K. "A cognitively oriented concept of piano technique," *Dissertation Abstracts* 47:114A July, 1986.

Principles of psycho-physiology are coordinated into a unified system of piano technique which stresses performance goals rather than body movements.

Brigard, Nancy and Sherwyn Woods. "Memory Problems for Musical Performers," *College Music Symposium* 18:102–09 n2 1978.

Most "memory losses" during performance are actually the result of failure in auditory concentration.

Camp, Max W. *Developing Piano Performance, A Teaching Philosophy* (Chapel Hill, NC: Hinshaw Music, 1981).

Designed as a textbook for university level pedagogy courses. Historical review of pedagogical approaches. Consideration of piano study vis-à-vis developmental learning theories.

Chapman, Norman. "A Treasury of Practice Devices," *Clavier* 6:19–20 n8 1967.

A list of variations, emphases, and devices to increase stimulation and concentration while practicing.

Ciccolini, Aldo. "Mental Practice," *Etude* 71:16+ September, 1953.

Maintains new pieces should be memorized before playing, with fingerings, attacks, tone, etc. planned in advance.

Collins, Richard. *Piano Playing, A Positive Approach* (Lanham, MD:University Press of America, 1986).

Stresses receptivity to "inner guidance" in practicing and playing, and urges stronger reliance on learning music "by ear" rather than just by the fingers.

Crain, Anthony J. "Memory as applied to piano," *Music Journal* 28:32 + n2 1970.

Stresses importance of careful fingering in memorization and suggests the desirability of a college-level course in memorizing.

Crowder, Louis. "Tone-the Outdated Controversy," *Clavier* 3:17–20 n2 1964.

Discusses (with pictures) details of the piano action and its effect on timbre, loudness, duration, etc.

———. "What is Style?," *Clavier* 5:20–21 n4 1966.

Discusses variation in style characteristics in playing music of the major composers. Includes suggestions concerning rubato, tempo, pedaling, tonal quality, and dynamic range.

———. "Piano Tone: The Outdated Controversy", *Clavier* 29:20–27 + n9 1990.

This slightly abridged version of the 1964 article emphasizes that the only forms of control pianists actually exert over tone color are the speed with which the hammer strikes the string and the blending of simultaneous tones.

Delzell, J.K. "Guidelines for a balanced performance schedule," *Music Educators Journal* 74:34–8 April, 1988.

Suggests that too many performances in school music programs may interfere with real music making.

DeVan, William and Carolyn Maxwell. "Preparing Students for Competition," *Clavier* 26:34–36 n4 1987.

Four relevant areas discussed are technique, repertoire, experience, and musicianship.

DeVinney, Richard. "Practice Planning Your Practice," *Clavier* 6:17–18 n8 1967.

Spending a few minutes each day in planning your practice will facilitate learning.

Elder, Dean. *Pianists at Play* (Evanston, IL: The Instrumentalist Co., 1982).

This pianist, teacher, and consulting editor for *Clavier* presents interviews with 26 pianists, master lessons on specific pieces of literature, and "technical regime interviews" with five great piano pedagogues.

Evans, Marsha M. "The Best Seat in the House," *American Music Teacher* 39:14–15 + n4 1990.

Describes the duties of an orchestra pianist and praises the excitement and opportunities of the position. Also includes a brief history of piano in the symphony orchestra.

Facko, R.I. "Remedial sight-reading for the college piano major," *Dissertation Abstracts* 32:668A August, 1971.

Suggestions for practice techniques and sequential examples from piano literature to improve college-level sight-reading.

Fenker, Richard. *Stop Studying, Start Learning* (Fort Worth, TX: Tangram Press, 1981).

Useful descriptions of techniques for muscle relaxation, mental programming, overcoming distractions, and generally improving learning behaviors.

Foldes, Andor. *Keys to the Keyboard. A Book for Pianists* (New York: E.P.Dutton, 1948).

Comments by a mid-century virtuoso on technique, practice, memorizing, and performance. Question and answer section.

Freyhan, Michael. "Reaching for the Chamber Music Ideal," *Piano Quarterly* 38: 34–37 n151 1990.

Reviews the differences between performing on the piano and on stringed instruments, and suggests ways to improve balance, intonation, and helpful cooperation between the players.

Gieseking, Walter and Karl Leimer. *Piano Technique* {New York: Dover, 1972}.

Emphasis on critical self-hearing and apprehension of the coherent musical structure as basis of technique.

Glazer, Gilda. "Training the Pianist as an Ensemble Player," *American Music Teacher* 16:28–29 n5 1967.

Professional training of pianists should include ensemble skills: sight-reading, score-reading while playing, rhythmic competence, and knowledge of the ensemble literature.

Gore, Virginia. "Sight-Reading for Pianists," *American Music Teacher* 27:7 n5 1978.

Some specific recommendations for building sight-reading proficiency.

Gross, Gail. "T'ai Chi Ch'uan in the Art of Piano Practice," *Piano Quarterly* 38: 53–56 n148 1989–90.

The Chinese Taoist exercises of T'ai Chi Ch'uan utilize essential qualities that pianists need to incorporate into their practicing: slowness, lightness, clarity, calmness, and balance.

Hacha, Barbara. "Preparing the High School Musician for College," *Clavier* 21:28–29 n3 1982.

Author finds most college first year piano students ill-prepared in theory, ear-training, sight-singing, sight-reading (piano), memorization, musical literature, performing experience, and independent work habits.

Haug, Sue. "Sight Playing and Visual Perception: The Eyes Have It," *American Music Teacher* 40: 22–23 + n3 1990–91.

Recent research on eye movements while sight playing changes some common misconceptions and suggests new strategies for improving this skill.

Hinson, Maurice. "Does Your Practice Make Perfect?," *American Music Teacher* 15:20–21 n1 1965.

A "checklist" of twenty-one suggestions on how to achieve efficient, concentrated, meaningful practice.

Hodges, Donald A. "Ten Teaching Tips Based on Brain Research," *Texas Music Teacher* 28:16+ n3 1989.

New understanding of the brain demonstrates validity of mental practice, slow repetitions for building motor skills, approaching concepts through several sensory modes.

Houston, Robert E. "Playing on Borrowed Time: A Brief History of Rubato," *American Music Teacher* 38:22–23+ n1 1988.

The origins, development, misconceptions, and twentieth-century interpretation of the term "rubato".

Hudson, W. Eugene. "Practice Makes Perfect-or Does It?", *Clavier* 16:48–50 n5 1977.

Practice techniques examined for their efficacy.

Janis, Byron. "The Fine Art of Practicing," *Etude* 67:9–10 October, 1949.

Each pianist should create exercises for the weaknesses of his own hands (and other useful practice suggestions).

Kapell, William. "Technique and Musicianship," *Etude* 68:20–21 December, 1950.

Need for technical work to be made as musical as possible. Also recollections of Samaroff's memorable teaching of musicianship.

Kungle, Sandra. "Self-Reliance for Rhythm and Tempo: Beyond Metronomic Dictates," *American Music Teacher* 37:24+ n3 1988.

Relation of rhythmic awareness to the muscular sense of physical pulse and motion.

Lewis, Martha R. "How to Teach Sight-Reading," *Clavier* 28:31–32 n7 1989.

Includes suggestions for sight-reading materials to be used in daily practice.

Lhevinne, Josef. *Basic Problems in Pianoforte Playing* (New York: Dover, 1972).

Insights from a master on touch, phrasing, accuracy, memorizing, etc.

Lo, L.N. "The effect of visual memory training on the ability to memorize music within class period instruction," *Dissertation Abstracts* 38:538A-39A August 1977.

In a class situation, visualizing the score with closed eyes induced concentration and aided the memorization of four-part harmonic keyboard material.

Marcus, Adele. *Great Pianists Speak* (Neptune, NJ: Pagininiana, 1979).

Marcus interviews eight pianists on their approaches to study and performance. Comments on learning new works are especially interesting.

Magrath, Jane. "Nerves, Memory, and Pianos," *American Music Teacher* 32:17–18 n6 1983.

The best remedy for nervousness is concentration on the music during practice and performance.

Manduca, Liz. "The Athletic Pianist," *Clavier* 24:19–21 n7 1985.

Compares piano practicing to athletics, suggesting activities and attitudes for warm-up, "the game" itself, cool-down, and between "games".

Sr. Mary Madeleine. "The College Piano Major," *Musart* 18:12–13 + n4 1966.

Outline of a four-year course of study which teaches technique and musical style in a weekly class along with private lessons.

Moffat, Joan B. "Pedaling, An Art and a Science," *Clavier* 25:18–21 n3 1986.

A series of pedaling exercises simulating styles that are found in the repertoire.

Moore, Gerald. *The Unashamed Accompanist* (London: Methuen and Co., 1959).

Treats many aspects of an accompanist's work, and preparation for this career.

————. *Am I Too Loud, a musical autobiography* (New York: MacMillan, 1962).

The personal and professional memoirs of one of the twentieth century's leading accompanists.

Mullins, Shirley Strohm. "So You Want to be an Accompanist!", *Clavier* 28: 48–50 n7 1989.

Strategies for getting established as an accompanist: give a free recital, contact schools and private music teachers, join musical organizations, etc.

Nagel, Louis B. "Overcoming Performance Anxiety," *Clavier* 24:22–23 n7 1985.

Practice techniques to overcome the chief causes of performance anxiety: possibilities of memory slips and of technical collapse.

Nagy, Bela. "Must it be memorized?," *Clavier* 4:20–23 n1 1965.

Advocates not enforcing memorization at the expense of repertoire; describes a technique for memorizing away from the keyboard.

Newman, William S. *The Pianist's Problems* (New York: Harper & Row, 1950).

A unified approach to the essential principles of technique, practice, historical styles, and musicianly playing.

Noyle, Linda J. *Pianists on Playing: Interviews with Twelve Concert Pianists* (Metuchen, NJ: Scarecrow Press, 1987).

Author interviews twelve pianists ranging in age from Rudolph Firkušný (born 1912) to André Michel-Schub, (born 1952) asking the same fifteen questions on the pianist's craft (practicing, memorizing, performing, etc.)

Prevatt, Harriet L. "Are You Running on Empty?," *Clavier* 29: 35 n6 1990.

Teachers of the piano must maintain their performing skills to remain fulfilled and inspiring musicians.

Price, Deon Nielsen. "Group Instruction in Accompanying," *Clavier* 20:30–36 n9 1981.

Techniques for teaching accompanying in various group situations such as lecture-demonstrations, workshops, short introductory courses, and semester-length college-level courses.

————. "The Special Skills of an Accompanist," *Clavier* 17:37–41 n7 1978.

Five needed skills of a vocal accompanist (pianistic, listening, interpretive, rehearsal, and performance) and how to acquire them.

Robert, Walter. "Achieving Relaxation thru Exercises," *Clavier* 12:22–23 n6 1973.

A group of exercises calculated to produce relaxation through control of rhythm and accent.

————. "Fingering," *Clavier* 12:8–13 n2 1973.

Principles behind fingering of scales, arpeggios, chords, and non-technical passage-work.

Rogers, George L. "The Bachelor of Music Degree and the Marketplace," *College Music Symposium* 28:106–16, 1988.

Given the state of the marketplace, the need to shift emphasis away from the B.M. to other music degrees.

Samaroff, Olga. "Accuracy in Musical Performance," *Musical Courier* 149:32–34 n11 1954.

A plea for training piano students toward musical independence in approaching scores of all periods.

Schick, Robert D. *The Vengerova System of Piano Playing* (University Park: Pennsylvania State University Press, 1982).

Description of Vengerova pedagogical system of accents, fingering, etudes, etc.

Schmied, Al. "The Importance of Developing Kinesthetic (Finger) Memory in Piano Performance," *The American Music Teacher* 23:11–12 n5 1974.

Practicing difficult passages with closed eyes improves control of spatial formations, and strengthens inner listening.

Schoenberg, Arnold. "How Can a Music Student Earn a Living?", *American Music Teacher* 38:25–26 n5 1989.

Famed composer lists remunerative occupations for a music student related to his work: music copyist and proofreader, arranger, accompanist, coach, teacher, salesman, and apprentice in a publishing house or recording studio.

Schuman, Judith. "Remedial Sight-Reading," *Clavier* 8:29–31 n2 1969.

Suggests teaching sight-reading in small classes, concentrating on correction of eye movement and improved tactile keyboard perception.

Shockley, Rebecca. "A 'Backward' Approach to Learning Music," *American Music Teacher* 36:32–33 n4 1987.

Methodology and psychological validity of memorizing music starting at the end of a composition.

Sivak, Tom. "Playing in the Pit," *Clavier* 30:36–38 n1 1991.

Playing for musical theater productions offers good job opportunities and requires excellent sight-reading plus a strong, well-articulated technique.

Slenczynska, Ruth. "Added color from special pedal techniques," *Clavier* 8:19–20 n2 1969.

Use of Prokofieff's *Visions Fugitives*, opus 22, as basis for pedal studies.

————. *Music at Your Fingertips* (New York: Da Capo Press, 1968).

Many helpful comments on practicing and program building, including rhythmic exercises, repertoire lists, and ornamentation charts.

Solomon, Judith. "The Pianist as Vocal Accompanist, Servant or Partner?," *Journal of Research in Singing* 13:55–65 n2 1990.

Stresses equality of accompanist with singer in performance and gives an overview of skills needed to be a professional accompanist.

Starker, Janos. "Partner, not Accompanist," *Clavier* 21:18–19 n9 1982.

Famous cellist underlines equal importance of pianist in ensemble music.

Strauman, Edward. "Managing Practice Time," *Piano Quarterly* 32:40–41 n125 1984.

How to maximize practice time by proper planning and the avoidance of negative thinking (boredom, procrastination, perfectionism, etc.).

Street, Eric. "Bridging the Gap Between Sight-Reading and Memorizing," *American Music Teacher* 37:32–33 n2 1987.

Author notes that most pianists develop as *either* good sight-readers *or* memorizers, and suggests methods for strengthening both skills.

Sturm, Jonathan A. "Are Conservatory Students Prepared to Enter the Higher Education Profession?," *American Music Teacher* 40:24–25 + n4 1991.

Conservatories should create workshops for their students to inform them about the musical climate of jobs in higher education; colleges should also give this type of information to conservatory trained job candidates.

Tommasini, Anthony. "Knowing the Score," *Piano Quarterly* 36:48–53 n142 1988.

The tradition of compulsory memorization of concert music by solo pianists may be changing. Gilbert Kalish, chairman of performance at SUNY, Stony Brook, believes that memorizing limits repertoire and may result in mechanical performance.

Van Auken, Richard and Paul Larson. "Teaching Inner Hearing," *American Music Teacher* 37:17 + n5 1988.

A training sequence presented which leads students to imagine the music as it should sound, then compare their performance with inner hearing.

Viviano, Samuel. "The Metronome, Its Use and Misuse," *American Music Teacher* 37:28 n1 1987.

Excellent short discussion of how to use the metronome to help develop the inner sense of pulse.

———. "Some Thoughts on Memorization," *American Music Teacher* 36:52 n2 1986.

One page summary of a workable process for memorizing.

Wagner, Jeffrey and Corey Kaup. "Record Yourself at the Piano," *Clavier* 28:17–20 n7 1989.

Recording is a useful tool for audition or teaching purposes. Important factors in a successful product are: the room, the piano, quality of tapes and tape deck, selection of microphones and their placement.

Yu, Benjamin B.M. "Mental Study in Piano Teaching," *American Music Teacher* 33:12–14 n6 1984.

Distinguished Chinese pedagogue advocates mental analysis of new scores before playing them; also mentally hearing and visualizing works already memorized.

PART III   SYNTHESIS

THE "WHY?" OF PERFORMANCE

The coming together of all the pianist's physical and mental activities charted above creates a "gestalt," i.e. a whole or combined entity known as performance. In so many instances, it is, indeed, the excitement and satisfaction of youthful pianistic performance which has been the earliest incentive for many musical lives that eventually develop toward teaching, conducting, musicology, and other non-performing careers. Yet few of those whose "paths diverged" (à la Robert Frost) ever completely abandon the first and purest joy of all:-that of re-creating the notes of a musical score with one's own fingers on the keyboard.

Happy beyond belief, then, should be the men and women for whom concert preparation and performance constitute a major portion of the daily work. And for the most part, this is so, especially for those artists who do not view their performing merely as a vehicle for the satisfaction of ego needs, but rather as an opportunity to share their own gifts, and those of the composers, with the rest of humanity. It must, however, be acknowledged that some playing situations which involve comparative evaluation (such as university "juries", lower-level contests , and major competitions), by their very nature tend to distort the delicate balance of the pianist's psychological focus. The best way to *keep* one's focus under this kind of pressure is to view every opportunity to play as a *performance*, and every gathering of listeners, be they faculty members, fellow pianists, or judges, as an *audience,* who can and will be reached by our musical communication.[1]

There are many specific things that can be done by a performer to ensure that he will emerge upon the concert stage in a state of readiness, relaxation, and pleasantly excited anticipation. Some of these go back through years of training, some pertain to the months and weeks before a performance, and some are directed at the very day and/or evening of the concert itself. In the writer's view, concertizing is like childbirth, in that the proper preparation can make all the difference between a painful, fear-ridden experience and a joyfully creative one.

THE "WHERE?" OF PERFORMANCE

Recitals and Competitions

Obviously, a paramount principle in the training of all would-be musical performers is to create as many opportunities as possible to play for audiences of all types and sizes. Most pianists will have their earliest performing experiences in their teacher's studio recitals, and in many cases, the young student's positive or negative response to this exposure will indicate to him (as well as to teachers and parents) whether or not there is a piano in his future.

As the student progresses, the teacher may begin to present him in partial or full recitals of his own. He may also start to enter some of the many contests which are now proliferating in this country, such as those sponsored by the Music Teachers' National Association, University Interscholastic League (for middle and high-school level), Piano Guild, and so on. A number of orchestras in the United States sponsor Young Artists' auditions, where advanced high-school students compete to play a concerto with the symphony, and there are also numerous workshops and clinics where students perform for and are evaluated by master teachers.

Again, a warning must be sounded as regards the individual student's psychological reaction to the atmosphere of competition which has increasingly come to surround all arts activities of our present day. Some young pianists are motivated to do their best work only through the challenge of competing with their peers, but if this is so, it must be emphasized that the most important goal is not winning the medal, the prize money, etc., but the ability to play the music with the greatest facility and insight. On the other hand, the promising student who does not bloom in a competitive setting should be exposed to as much recital and accompanying work as possible, until his playing is mature enough for a decision to be made as to its direction. There are many pianists in the field today who have built performing careers without ever having entered a single contest, and, conversely, competition winners are not automatically ensured of careers.

It must be underlined that competitions are one road to a performing goal, but *only* one. Increasingly, the business-oriented and political aspects of competitions are coming in for examination and criticism by people like Ellen Cline (Dean of the Peabody Institute) in her articles in *American Music Teacher*[2] and Joseph Horowitz, the respected music critic, in *The Ivory Trade,* a revealingly detailed chronicle of the Van Cliburn Competition.[3] Even Abbey Simon, one of the most sought after competition judges of the current scene, feels that the system may have expanded to the point of diminishing returns:

> Contests are contests at this point, he says, and they have, in a way, come to the end of their usefulness. . . . The point is that it is getting completely out of hand. I think what we really need are national competitions, with one big international competition held every four or five years comprised of the winners of the national competitions.[4]

So, it seems, the winds of change may be rising. Aspiring young pianists will have to remain flexible and observe which way they blow.

Organizations

There are many school organizations that provide a fertile field for young pianists to begin playing in public and with other people. (This is a type of experience which will prove useful, and sometimes lucrative, regardless of whether a solo or ensemble career is anticipated). By middle and/or high-school, enough skill may have been acquired to begin putting it to use as accompanist for various choral groups, or for school orchestras which will often use a pianist if one is available. Other instrumentalists and singers in the organization will then seek out these able pianists to accompany them, in many audition, contest, and performing situations.

The same opportunities will continue to present themselves in a college or conservatory setting. Also, by now, the pianist may begin to accompany in the studios of vocal and instrumental faculty, and thereby to come in contact with singers and players with whom he will perform in recital the masterpieces of vocal literature and chamber music.

Besides school organizations, there are many community organizations that sponsor contests and/or invite young musicians to provide musical programs for their meetings. Under this heading may be found musical and literary clubs, and service organizations such as Rotary, Kiwanis, Business and Professional Women, etc. The atmosphere at these meetings is usually very receptive to and appreciative of developing players, and is a nurturing setting in which to practice the art of performance.

Since these club meetings will take place in hotel ballrooms, restaurants, and other such settings out and around town, it is essential that the pianist check into the type and condition of the instrument that he will be called upon to play. To avoid last minute surprises, the best plan is to request a rehearsal time at least two days prior to performance, so that tuning can be done if needed or other negative situations rectified if possible. Sometimes improvement is *not* possible, in which case the pianist may choose to either decline the engagement, or at least be forewarned as to his performing conditions.

Churches and Synagogues

The liturgical setting is a fruitful performing situation for pianists, even those who are not drawn to the organ as an alternate instrument. Indeed, many small churches cannot afford organs, and are happy to have young pianists practice their skills by playing hymns, accompanying the choir and vocal soloists, and airing their own solo repertoire as preludes, offertories, and postludes.

Synagogues are less likely to need pianists for services since Orthodox and Conservative worship exclude instruments, and Reform congregations traditionally use an organ. But religious schools are often looking for pianists to help the children prepare programs or learn Sabbath and holiday songs, and some synagogues maintain children's choirs which use accompanists.

Many of the larger churches and synagogues have performing spaces and pianos that are eminently suited for concert presentations, and are open to sponsoring recitals by well-prepared young musicians. Often they will provide publicity, programs, and an established audience, all of which makes this a highly desirable location for either a principal or "try-out" performance.

One of the major psychological benefits in the liturgical setting, to a pianist in need of performance exposure, is the opportunity it affords to submerge the ego, and its related tensions, in the service of a spiritual purpose. In the author's experience, many able students of the piano, who suffer performance anxiety, have been able to break through to a comfort level of public playing, as a result of numerous Sundays spent on the piano bench of a neighborhood church. This ease in performing can then be carried over to other areas, as can, one would hope, the attitude of service, which is a highly productive and energizing state of mind.

Musical Theater

Another and different arena in which pianists are constantly in demand, and where they can further hone their performing skills, is that of musical theater. An able young pianist will often begin in high-school productions to accompany rehearsals and performances of Gilbert and Sullivan operettas or some selection from the extensive American musical comedy repertoire. He may well continue to do so for college or conservatory theaters, and by this time may be sufficiently skilled to take on operatic scores for the opera workshop productions that are common on the university level.

As his experience and competence increase, the pianist may be invited, often for sizable fees, to serve as music director for local community productions of musical theater. This position usually involves accompanying, coaching, some degree of conducting (if only from the piano), and a greater or lesser involvement with the hiring of orchestral players and the casting of the singing roles. Some pianists are able to finance a fair portion of their advanced studies by taking on one or two shows in summer vacation, or even during the school term if the demanding theatrical schedules can be made workable with their class and practice responsibilities.

Occasionally, a pianist who finds he has a flair for conducting (or composing and arranging), and who is excited by the dramatic situation, may make a career in musical theater. Even if this does not occur, the opportunity the work affords to gain control of a complex musical ensemble, as well as the handling of intricate human relations, will prove invaluable for all later career choices.

Friends

The cultivation of a wide circle of musical friends is not only useful to the developing pianist, but inspirational as well, since peer approval and support are essential to all young people, and the emerging musician is no exception.

These friends are most likely to be encountered within musical organizations such as choirs and orchestras, sponsored by the public schools or by churches. Some communities also support youth choruses or instrumental groups that admit the most talented by audition. Coming together, then, through a common interest, young musicians readily form supportive friendships, and a pianist will come to know a number of singers, and string and wind players, with whom he can play the vocal and chamber works, and for whom he can perform his solo repertoire.

The act of performing, and the psychological conditions predisposing to performance anxiety, need to be practiced. By the time sated family members are weary of the repertoire, musical friends constitute the logical alternative for a rehearsal audience. The request will not be seen as burdensome since reciprocity will be expected, and the feedback will be knowledgeable, therefore welcome-a productive undertaking for all concerned.

A still further extension of playing for friends is imagining their presence, plus whoever else might be the most anxiety-producing for the pianist. Louis B. Nagel suggests that one "visualize a performance situation. . . . Imagine the hall, stage, audience, microphones, whatever images that will arouse nervousness, and then perform the program. This nerve-vaccine will help enormously",[5] and a booster shot of it can be taken when friends are unavailable.

As a Singer

This heading may prove somewhat surprising, but in the writer's opinion, it is extremely valuable for a pianist to gain as much experience as possible in using his own voice, whether as a member of a school, church, or community chorus, or by cultivating the solo repertoire in a vocal studio.

As suggested in an earlier section, this training will prove useful, first of all in a coaching situation where pianists are called upon to check singers' pitches, pay attention to (although not to correct) vocal production, and sometimes even to sing the missing parts when an operatic role is being prepared. Equally important is the pianist's degree of comfort with using his own voice in counting aloud and in following the motivic line, while practicing, and especially memorizing his solo repertoire. The best way to stay with the music is to hear it, and the surest way to hear it is to sing it. Glenn Gould's incredible artistry, accompanied by his ubiquitous "singing", is the clearest proof of the results of this kind of focusing. All pianists need to sing more, and teachers need to start their students on this path as early as possible, before socially learned embarrassment begins to hinder this most natural of responses.

PREPARATION FOR PERFORMANCE

Synthesis Observed

In selecting program material and preparing it for performance, the promised synthesis of bodily and mental faculties can be seen to be operating at its highest level. As the fingers continue to be trained for ever-increasing facility, they will be useless without the musical concepts which the mind chooses to present. Further, program building will necessitate an intelligent assessment of the player's physical capacities, and *Lancet,* the British medical journal, comments on this from the physician's viewpoint:

> The strains placed on a pianist's hands vary considerably from composer to composer," it states. "Small hands will prove inadequate for the large stretches required by Rachmaninov and Liszt; long fingers seem cramped on the passage work of Mozart.[6]

Yet another aspect of this synthesis will involve bodily responses, usually not consciously controlled, to the emotional content or style period of the repertoire. In the case of emotional response, the pianist must guard against exaggerated swaying, jumping, head nodding, and grimacing, which in moderation may add conviction to his performance, but in excess will surely detract from it. This warning is especially important in an ensemble situation, since few singers or instrumentalists will agree to be consistently upstaged by an over-athletic pianist. On the other hand, a "stone statue" of a pianist can be equally off-putting to an audience, so a middle ground must be found, wherein small alterations of upper torso position, head carriage, and facial expression may satisfy the player's need for dramatic corroboration without disturbing the artistic balance.

The concept of bodily adjustment to stylistically appropriate performance is, however, a totally different matter, and one which must be thoroughly mastered by pianists seeking a mature level of performance. The fact is that the fingers, wrists, arms, and shoulders will be used quite differently depending on the designated period of musical interpretation. Baroque repertoire, for instance, will emphasize finger movement, with a pointed, focused attack by a small area of the finger pad. Romantic music, seeking a warmer sound, will involve greater use of flexible wrist movements, arms, and shoulders for weight transfer, and a larger area of the finger pad clinging to the keys for a greater semblance of legato. Twentieth-century music will achieve its harsh brilliance through much percussive striking of the keys, while the Classic period approach will fall between the Baroque and Romantic.

Pianists who are given an opportunity to perform on the harpsichord will find that their body use must be modified further to adapt to this instrument, whose plucked quill mechanism does not respond to varying degrees of pressure on the keys, or to any use whatever of wrists, arms, and shoulders. Necessary for this instrument is the cultivation of great precision in striking both single notes and chords through the employment of a very pointed finger attack. Keyboard players may, in fact, find it preferable not to concertize on both piano and harpsichord in a single program if possible, since the technical demands are so different.

In playing the harpsichord, the pianist will also have to adapt to the absence of pedals as he knows them. (Some harpsichords do have an organ-type pedal board, and others, a few pedals that control coupling of registers). In general, most pianists can benefit from some degree of separate vacation from their damper pedal and the opportunity the separation affords to further develop manual legato and smoothness of connection in passage work.

In regard to the use of the pedal in piano music, however, the author agrees with Ernst Bacon in his insightful book, *Notes on the Piano,* concerning the desirability of tasteful pedaling in all periods of the repertoire, and in all but the very earliest stages of learning a new work. The composer herein reminds us of the obviously true, but often ignored, fact that the position of dampers lifted from strings constitutes the natural state of the piano, and that over-dryness is, therefore, a distortion of true piano sound. He also solves the ever-present dilemma of whether to pedal Baroque compositions with the following lucid comments:

> The clavichord and the harpsichord. . . . were more perfectly suitable for the playing of polyphonic music, since they could allow successive harmonies to run into each other without clouding, yet suffered not the dryness of the unpedalled piano. In polyphonic music, the piano must artfully *compromise* between the dryness of non-pedalling, and the enriching of harmony with continuous pedalling. The greatest confusion has resulted from the notion that, because the Bachian clavichord had no pedal, the piano should eschew its use in the music of that time.[7]

One final observation on stylistically appropriate performance seems indicated here. Whether by virtue of physical characteristics, personality, musical taste, or all of the foregoing, no pianist is equally enamored of or suited to all areas of the enormous keyboard literature. If he is being hired as an orchestral musician or an accompanist, he must of course play what has been programmed, but where, as a soloist or chamber player, he has a voice in the selection of repertoire, he would do well to listen to the words of Rudolph Firkušný, the great Czechoslovakian pianist:

> There are certain things", says Firkušný, "which I don't play. It's not because I don't know the music, but I somehow feel that I have no affinity for the piece. . . . But then, thank God, we have so much repertoire that we can always be choosy, which is a great privilege.[8]

Learning the Program

Once the program has been selected, a learning schedule should be constructed. It should be designed so as to insure the fullest cooperation of the mind and body in the demanding intellectual and physical tasks about to be undertaken by the brain and fingers.

Goals should be set for the learning and memorizing of each piece, given a realistic assessment of available practice time, that will enable the maintenance of good physical and mental health. In constructing a learning schedule, one must take into account one's own bio-rhythms, and plan memorizing sessions for those times when mental energies are at their highest. Ernst Bacon, again, has useful, and indeed, poetic advice on this subject:

> Morning is for labor, afternoon for routine, and evening for the imagination. These may vary, but experience shows that the critical and energetic faculties come soonest after rest; while the mind is dullest in mid-day; and evening is when the spirit is mellowest, and most charitable to new thoughts.[9]

It must also be kept in mind that memorizing can be done away from a piano (such as during bus or plane travel) by working visually with a score. There are, in fact, tales abroad of many a famous pianist who, in former eras, memorized an entire concerto for a performance which followed upon a cross-country train trip.

If the concert in question involves a singer or other instrumentalist(s), the same type of scheduling must be undertaken but with some differences. Now the pianist must, in effect, create two separate schedules. The first of these charts his own practice time which will be spent, not only in learning his own music thoroughly, but also in becoming very conversant with the singer's vocal line and text, or the parts to be performed by the other chamber players. A decision also needs to be made fairly early on as to whether or not a page turner will be used in the concert, since a pianist turning his own pages will have to practice these movements as an integral part of the performance. In the writer's opinion, the pianist should always be prepared to turn for himself, since the uncertainties of performance, especially out-of-town, often make this unavoidable.

At this point, when he would be memorizing if it were a solo program, he must now begin a series of rehearsals with his musical partner(s). These must be sufficient in number so that ample time will be allowed to develop a secure ensemble, and to arrive at a mutually satisfactory interpretation of the repertoire.

A handy "rule of thumb" for programming newly learned music is that it should be thoroughly memorized or otherwise prepared by one month (at the very least) before the concert. Now it is time to begin taking it out of the practice studio and moving it into the hall and onto the instrument where it will actually be performed. Often this will prove to be quite a shock, initially, as the performer begins to deal with all the vagaries of a different piano, and all the distractions of an unfamiliar setting. This, of course, is the very reason that a month before is none too soon to begin adjusting to the new conditions, with the eventual goal of ignoring them and returning to the desired concentration on the music.

Acoustical aspects of the concert hall are another important factor which must be addressed in these final rehearsals. Often it may be hard for the pianist to judge accurately what he is projecting by way of dynamics and tone, and it is here that another pair of ears—a teacher's or a musical colleague's—may be invaluable. Many stages are constructed so that the sound is larger to the audience than what the player hears himself, and this can result in forcing and bodily strain if unrecognized. Further, it is almost always impossible to judge matters of balance between chamber players or between singer and accompanist from behind the footlights. Knowledgeable advice on the required position of the piano lid and placing of the performers on the stage is therefore indispensable.

The writer is well aware that the notion of a month's "lead time" in a concert-hall may, in many cases, be the purest fantasy. Indeed, a pianist playing an out-of-town recital may be lucky to succeed in spending a few hours with his instrument and hall, sandwiched hectically between arrival and performance. Whatever the cost in travel arrangements, these few hours are minimally essential, and can in no way be surrendered, and the same is true of a listener's judgment as to the balance of an ensemble. A professional ear is, of course, most desirable, but a husband, wife, manager, host, or hostess can prove a useful substitute when necessary.

Concert Clothes

At some point during the final month of preparation, the subject of concert attire needs to be addressed. There are numerous decisions to be made in this area and they are important, because a jarring or inappropriate visual image can diminish the favorable impact on an audience of a positive aural experience.

The performer should first take into consideration the season of the year, part of the country, and probable temperature of the concert stage when selecting materials to be worn. A heavily air-conditioned hall in a Texas summer might be cooler than steam-heated December in New York, so one either acquires beforehand information on the situation, or plans to be ready for anything. This readiness will involve bringing choices of shirt and jacket weight for a man, and layers that can be added or switched for a woman.

Comfort, of course, is paramount, since anything else will prove distracting. Pianists should be sure that their shoulders and neck are not restricted, that sleeves are not too long, and that rings or other types of jewelry are not heavy or obtrusive. Shoes should be comfortable and well-fitting, and women need to be certain that the heel height is manageable for purposes of pedalling. Indeed, the whole concert outfit should be tried out in the playing situation, and, optimally, rehearsed in for a period of time.

Appropriateness of dress to the nature of the programmed material is another consideration which can add visual interest. It is no longer considered mandatory for performers to appear in tail coats or very formal gowns, although this still tends to be the norm for most solo recitals and concerto appearances with orchestra. Ensemble groups specializing in contemporary music are beginning to wear colorful blouses and pants for men and women, performers of music by Latin-American composers may choose Fiesta-like attire, and so on. The door has been opened in recent years to more imaginative choices in this aspect of concert planning.

One rule of dress, however, which must be followed, is that members of a performing ensemble (meaning anything greater than one person) need to coordinate their planning. This is necessary to ensure that colors, style, degree of formality, etc. present a united and complementary picture to the audience. In the case of a female accompanist to a singer (be the vocalist male or female), the writer suggests wearing black unless expressly invited to do otherwise. The world being as it is, an accompanist who upstages the soloist, through ignorance or through intent, is unlikely to be rehired.

Securing One's Audience

Every performer dreams of a hall that is filled to overflowing on concert night without any foregoing effort on his part. Unfortunately, this dream becomes a reality for only a handful of the best known pianists at the peak of their careers. The rest of us have to work for our audiences by careful attention to the details of publicity, starting about one month before the date of performance.

If the concert is to be given as a faculty recital, the problem has a simple solution, as most colleges and universities have public relations departments which will handle news releases to local papers and arts calendars, and announcements to radio and television stations. In this situation, the pianist needs only to get the program material, biographical information, and pictures, if requested, to the appropriate persons in ample time for their appearance in the media.

If no such help is available, the performer is on his own. He should then transmit all the above information himself, by telephone or in writing. The latter is preferable, and in the case of the newspapers, the best plan is to hand carry one's material to the local music writers and critics, along with an in-person request for a concert review.

Another method of audience gathering which can be used in conjunction with the above, is to keep on hand a list of interested people who would be likely to come to one's concerts, and to send them individual postcards of announcement and invitation. If there is a friend or sponsoring organization who will produce a post-concert reception, it should be so indicated on the cards, since the chance to greet the performer in a social situation will be an added attendance incentive to many people.

Once everything has been set in place to inform the public of the event, the performer must let it go and concentrate only on his musical preparation. If it is extremely necessary to his future career that reviewers be present, he will need to court them with personal contacts and reminders. Otherwise, this possibility should also be forgotten, lest the prospect of critical evaluation constitute a block between the pianist and his pure communication with his audience.

Programs

Here again, we are addressing matters which may be handled by a university music department, public events office, or other sponsoring organization, but lacking any of these will need to be undertaken by the individual performer. If programs must be privately done, any print and copy shop can turn out an attractive product with choice of colors, print styles, etc. for a reasonable charge. In any case, all program copy, including repertoire, biographical sketches of performers, and notes on the composers or compositions, should be submitted at least three to four weeks in advance of the concert. This will allow for possible delays, and will also afford the opportunity for at least one proof-reading to correct the errors which invariably occur.

In the case of a vocal recital, song texts should unfailingly be provided for the audience. It is not necessary that they be printed with the programs, and can simply be typed and photo-copied, or whatever is the least expensive method. The important thing is that the audience be able to see the texts both before and during the recital, so that they can understand and follow the musical treatment of the poetry, which is the point of high excitement in the vocal literature. If there are foreign language texts, the originals should appear side by side with translations. Nor should English language poetry go unprinted, in the mistaken notion that it will be easily apprehended by the audience. Even if every singer's English vocal diction were perfect enough to make every word clearly audible (as is rarely the case), the poem still needs to be read and assimilated before the song is heard, in order for the composer's setting to be fully appreciated.

Recordings

Many colleges and universities have arrangements for routine recordings of musical events. Indeed, some "state of the art" concert halls now include built-in microphones which are monitored in the same booths that house the lighting controls. If the performer is responsible for his own recording (and these tapes can prove invaluable for learning and audition purposes), he must bring in either a friend whose work is of known quality, or else hire a professional. In the latter instance, it is important that the sound engineer be experienced in the recording of classical music, since the goals and processes are entirely different from what is desirable in popular recordings.

Although most recordings are made during the concert itself, it may be worth considering whether or not it would be more useful to record a dress rehearsal during concert week. The principal advantage to this is that a cleaner tape, without clapping, coughing, or other audience noise is thereby obtained. Another option that might be considered is to make one's own tapes before the concert so as to keep self-correcting from the information gained, and then to schedule the professional recording for a date shortly after the concert, when the repertoire is still fresh and the anxiety level abated. This latter plan is, of course, only possible if the same concert hall, or other location with suitable instrument and acoustics, is available as a recording site.

Tension and Anxiety

The reader is first of all referred back to the discussion called "From Body to Mind" in the opening section of the book. The important principles set forth therein can now be directly related to performance preparation, as we trace the connection between bodily tension and mental anxiety.

As originally suggested, this connection is not linear, but circular. The reader will also recall that music learned or memorized in a state of physical tension, with torso poorly supported and neck strained, will likely always be performed in the same condition of muscular tension. Each playing of these passages will then produce discomfort, loss of technical control, and anxiety, which will serve to increase muscular tension, eventually resulting in pain and disability.

It seems clear that the way to break this cycle of undesirable consequences is to conjoin the intellectual task of practice scheduling, which we have carefully detailed in chapters one to three, with the earlier recommendations in chapter one for good body use while practicing and performing. Taking care to monitor the body for good support and "released" muscles during all phases of pianistic learning is essential for developing relaxed control of performance. The pianist is also well-advised to check himself regularly in all other daily activities so that good body use becomes a lifetime habit.

The tension/anxiety cycle will also be dealt a lethal blow by the type of structured preparation and rehearsal scheduling we have described in the foregoing section. With sufficient preparation time, the pianist (and his colleagues) will be able either to ensure confident technical control, or to make program changes if the original choices prove unworkable. There is, in truth, no greater assurance a performer can carry on stage than the certain knowledge that he has done everything possible to prepare for this concert, and that another week's preparation would not materially improve his performance.

Positive reinforcement for the habit patterns we are attempting to establish on the piano bench can be gained by the adaptation of contemporary bio-feedback techniques. Before going to sleep at night, while doing Alexander Technique "lie-downs" (see chapter one), or in one of our daily breaks, we can practice progressive letting-go and tightening of each muscle group in succession until total bodily relaxation is achieved. At that point, we should begin to visualize ourselves in the concert situation—calm, confident, and in control—and to inwardly play through as much as possible of our music in this state. This type of inner programming for success has become standard in many areas of athletics, and musicians are now beginning to realize how applicable this body-mind process is to our needs and goals as well.

In this connection, the reader is again referred to Barry Green's evocative writing on "The Inner Game of Music," which game, he says, is about overcoming distractions that stand between us being at our best in . . . . performing. Distractions," he continues, "take the form of an inner voice attempting to control our actions and keep our attention away from the music. These diversions can be overcome by letting go to different aspects of the music.[10]

In our visualizations, then, we can see ourselves as letting go *of* the critical mind, of concern about mistakes, and even of the techniques of "the game" itself, while we let go *into* the sounds, imagery, and emotion of the music.

Two other weapons should be added to our arsenal in the war against tension and anxiety, and both are a matter of attitude. First, the successfully developing pianist must guard against unrealistic expectations for himself, and accept the fact that there is no such thing as perfection in performance. He should prepare so well that 80 to 90 percent of his best will constitute an acceptable level in concert, at the same time knowing that he may achieve more, or that one of the rehearsals may indeed prove to be the magical musical moment that makes the whole experience worthwhile.

Secondly, and perhaps most importantly, he must remember why he is performing (see *Motivation* in chapter two). Richard Miller points the way here, in a recent article directed to singers but equally applicable to pianists.

Performance," he tells us, "is an act of sharing, not of self-demonstration. The compelling recitalist is a mediator between the. . . . literature and the audience, like the person who shakes the beautiful little paper weight so that others may look in at the miniature scene of falling snow. . . . This performance quality is largely what separates the true artist from the showman. . . . When performance becomes an act of communication, rather than personal display or confrontation, performance anxiety greatly diminishes.[11]

This emotional focus can and should be practised during the positive visualization exercises, so that performing habit patterns will gradually become established for a properly directed and prepared mind in a comfortably energized body.

For those performers whose anxiety level remains incapacitatingly high up to the very hour of the concert (all types of preparation notwithstanding), the use of beta-blocking drugs to prevent the extreme effects of adrenalin release is a possibility to be considered. These effects are most likely to be pounding or palpitating heart, increased muscular contraction, and tremors. Because the last of these is crucially pertinent to bowing, string players have figured most prominently in trials of beta-blocking agents, with apparently favorable results in many cases.[12,13]

A pianist, whose tremors would be less obvious than those which produce a shaking bow, must carefully calculate the pros and cons of modifying the action of his adrenal glands. He must assess to what degree he is willing to accept a diminished level of nervous energy that the drug-induced slower heart-rate will produce, and he must measure it against the level of performance disability caused by his anxiety. A young, inexperienced performer may well find that the simple solution of playing in public more often may cause the symptoms to abate, and in the writer's opinion, all strategies of coping should be explored by the performer before the last resort of medication is essayed. In the event that the latter decision is made, the drugs must, under all circumstances, be prescribed and administered by a physician, as dosage level and selection of the optimal agent require professional direction.

PERFORMANCE

Just Before the Concert

An interesting phenomenon which the writer has observed many times in herself, in other performers, and in students, is the sensation of overwhelming fatigue which tends to occur sometime during the week before a concert.

This can be so strong that it feels like imminent illness, and leads to the not entirely unwelcome thought: "I'm sick; I'll never have the energy to play this concert; I'll have to cancel." It seems likely that this is a result of the great physical and emotional energies that are involved in the concert preparation and rehearsals, as well as a kind of physiological prelude to the release of adrenalin which will occur closer to the performance. Whatever the cause, the feeling should be recognized ("Ah, here it is again!"), and honored by lightening one's overall workload as much as possible and by paying special attention to the principles of body nurturance described above (rest, nutrition, exercise, etc.).

Nothing should be allowed to interfere with a full complement of sleep the night before the concert. Following that, the pianist should spend a quiet day which must include, preferably in the morning, an unhurried opportunity to play through all the music, not necessarily at performance energy level. This final run-through is really aimed less at the fingers than it is at the mind, since it is the last chance to gain reassurance as to the vivid presence of all details of the music in one's consciousness.

Again, teaching or other work-loads should be reduced or abandoned on concert day if at all possible, and even the presence of well-meaning friends or relatives who have traveled in for the event, should be discouraged until after the performance is over. Social conversation requires more energy than most people realize, and is experienced as an unwelcome distraction by most performers. It is highly preferable for the player to be alone with his slowly building focus toward communication, to sleep or rest for a period in the afternoon, and then to have a peaceful, light supper by himself or with someone who understands his state of inner preparation.

Ample time should be allowed for dressing (see *Concert Clothes* in previous section) which, depending on circumstances, can take place either at home or at the concert hall. After an unhurried trip, the pianist should arrive in time to look over the hall, and warm up briefly on stage before the audience begins to arrive. At this point, it is extremely useful to have someone else designated to check into details concerning programs, ushers, and readiness of equipment and personnel if the concert is to be recorded.

The pianist is now closeted somewhere backstage waiting for the concert to begin. Again, the necessity for social conversation should be avoided. Before-concert time should be divided in half, the first half to be spent in last minute communion with one's collaborator(s) or oneself on details of the music or performance. Then, after a mental acknowledgement that all possible outer preparation is over, the second half should be a quiet, calm, solitary process of *inner* preparation. During this time, the artist must see himself in the successful role of his, by now familiar, positive visualizations. He can also choose to inwardly dedicate the music to the composers who brought it into the world, to the audience with whom he will share it, or any more personal dedication that may have meaning to him.

Now it is curtain time and our pianist is fully ready. Knowing that all the work of preparation is over, and looking forward to an uninterrupted flow of what he is about to communicate, he can step joyfully and confidently onto the stage.

During the Concert

Once seated on the bench, he will take whatever time is necessary to mentally prepare each piece of music to be performed. This includes the drawing of several deep, centering breaths (remembering that the exhalation is particularly important to muscular relaxation) and the setting of an inner tempo by thinking through the first few measures of the work. If it is a chamber music concert, the pianist will, of course, have to be sensitive to the needs of all the other participants (tuning strings, releasing water from wind instruments, etc.), which may arise even between movements of a longer work. When accompanying an experienced singer, the pianist's role will be one of adapting to the other's timetable in dramatically preparing each song, whereas an inexperienced singer may have to be led and encouraged by the accompanist to take sufficiently restorative breaks between the sections of the program and the individual selections as well.

Intermission is only halfway through the concert, and should continue to be carefully controlled. Visits to the performer should be limited, and it would be highly desirable

Figure 7. " All the work of preparation is over."

if he could rest for five to ten minutes in the lying down "Alexander" position in which spinal extension does so much to restore energy. A short time spent in mental contact with the remaining music and a renewal of his dedicatory focus will then prepare the pianist for the "second half".

Last Words

The aftermath of a concert should be a joyous time of accepting congratulations from members of the audience and should never be marred by self-deprecating statements on the part of the performer (such as "I played better yesterday" or "Did you *hear* what happened in the first movement of the Mozart?"). All praise should be pleasantly received, and a simple "Thank you" will always suffice as a rejoinder. Parties or receptions (that the pianist did not have to arrange) are an excellent way to bring to closure the energies that will still be running at the end of the concert, although over-indulgence in food, drink, or late hours is inadvisable to anyone who wants to maintain his body in top performing condition.

With the appearance of the next day's newspapers, our pianist will have to deal either with the disappointment of absent or unfavorable reviews, or with the elation and consequent need to maintain perspective that favorable ones will produce. Unfortunately, there are very few so-called music critics in this country who are well-enough informed for their judgments to be considered expert testimony. That being the case, the writer's advice is to use a favorable review for publicity purposes, and to ignore an occasional unfavorable one, after first determining whether or not there is anything to be learned from it.

Expect "post-partum" depression after a concert. Very high energies have been geared to the birth of an artistic event, and feelings very akin to the obstetrically described "baby blues" will likely attend the letting down of those energies when it is all over. There is only one sure cure for this condition and that is, after a decent interval of rest and recuperation, to begin immediately planning for the next performance.

ENDNOTES FOR PART III

1. See Green, Barry. "Gaining Control by Letting Go: The Inner Game of Music," *American Music Teacher* 37:12–15 n3 1988.

2. Cline, Ellen T. "Anyone Can Win," *American Music Teacher* 40:24–27 n1 1990 and Cline, Ellen T. "Anyone Can Win, Round Two," *American Music Teacher* 40:28–31+ n1 1990.

3. See Horowitz, Joseph. *The Ivory Trade* (New York: Summit Books, 1990) and Horowitz, Joseph. "The Ivory Trade," *American Music Teacher* 40:18–21+ n3 1990–91 (excerpt from the above).

4. Abbey Simon in Noyle, Linda J. *Pianists on Playing* (Metuchen, NJ: Scarecrow Press, 1987), pp. 124–125.

5. Nagel, Louis B. "Overcoming Performance Anxiety," *Clavier* 24:22–23 n7 1985, p. 23.

6. "The Music Clinic," *Lancet* 1:1309–10 1985, p. 1310.

7. Bacon, Ernst. *Notes on the Piano* (Syracuse: Syracuse University Press, 1963), p. 52. Also see Banowetz, Joseph. *The Pianist's Guide to Pedalling* (Bloomington: Indiana University Press, 1985).

8. Rudolph Firkusny in Noyle, Linda J. *Pianists on Playing* (Metuchen, NJ: Scarecrow Press, 1987), p. 85.

9. Bacon, op. cit., p. 73.

10. Green, op. cit., p. 12.

11. Miller, Richard. "Is There a Cure for Performance Anxiety?," *The NATS Journal* 45:19–22 n1 1988, p. 22.

12. Liden, S. and C.Gottfries. "Beta-blocking agents in the treatment of catecholamine-induced symptoms in musicians," *Lancet* 2:529, 1974.

13. James, I.M., R.M.Pearson, D.N.M.Griffith, et al. "Effect of oxprenolol on stage-fright in musicians," *Lancet* 2:952–954, 1977.

BIBLIOGRAPHY FOR PART III

Appel, Sylvia S. "Modifying solo performance anxiety in adult pianists," *Journal of Music Therapy* 13:2–16 n1 1976.

Solo performance anxiety in adult pianists can be modified by systematic desensitization training.

Artesani, Laura. "Warm Up to Calm Down," *Clavier* 28:37–38 n5 1989.

Stresses the importance of a short, prepared warm–up for an audition or contest situation.

Bacon, Ernst. *Notes on the Piano* (Syracuse: Syracuse University Press, 1963).

Composer speaks as a pianist with insightful comments on preparation and performance.

Bernstein, Seymour. *With Your Own Two Hands* (New York: Schirmer Books, 1981).

Excellent contemporary treatment of many areas vital to the pianist (see Bibliographies for Parts I and II above).

Berumen, Ernesto. "High or Close Finger Action?," *Musical Courier* 142:39 n4 1950.

High fingers build strength and clarity, close fingers legato and warmth of tone. Both are needed.

Bonpensiere, Luigi. *New Pathways to Piano Technique* (New York: Philosophical Library, 1953).

Description of "Ideo-Kinesis" (see Bibliographies for Parts I and II above).

Boyd, Mary Boxall. "Between the Diploma and the Concert Stage," *Musical Courier* 156:6–7 n7 1957.

Schnabel's teaching assistant writes of the need to develop relaxed "body resilience" which enables technical ease and concentrated inner listening.

Brandfonbrenner, Alice G. "The Price of Perfection," *Medical Problems of Performing Artists* 3:1, 1988.

An editorial urging physicians to educate audiences about the price in stress and illness that performers pay in their "quest for perfection".

Brantigan, C.O., T.A.Brantigan, and N.Joseph. "Effect of Beta Blockade and Beta Stimulation on Stage-Fright," *American Journal of Medicine* 72:88–94, 1982.

Studies show that beta blockade eliminates stage fright problems while beta stimulating increases them. Comments on cultivation of stage-fright by our high-stress system of musical training (auditions, juries, etc.)

Bridges, A.K. "A cognitively oriented concept of piano technique," *Dissertation Abstracts* 47:114A July, 1986.

Principles of psycho-physiology are coordinated into a unified system of piano technique which stresses performance goals.

Brower, Harriette. *What to Play, What to Teach* (Philadelphia: Theodore Presser Co., 1925).

Selection of study and teaching material and the art of program building. Of value, although Granados and Scriabine are the most recent composers included.

Chase, Mildred Portnoy. *Just Being at the Piano* (Berkeley: Creative Arts Book Co., 1985).

Importance of pianist's sensory awareness, emotional experience, and centeredness in the present moment. (Foreword by Lee Strasberg finds relationships to his work in training actors).

Chasins, Abram. *Speaking of Pianists*, 3rd ed. (New York: Da Capo Press, 1981).

Third edition of a book first printed in 1961. This concert pianist shares recollections of his teachers, students, and fellow pianists, with many comments on the state of the pianistic art.

Cline, Ellen T. "Anyone Can Win," *American Music Teacher* 40:24–27 + n1 1990.

This study, based on hundreds of interviews and question-naires, traces the history, purpose, and politics of major performance competitions.

———. "Anyone Can Win, Round Two," *American Music Teacher* 40:28–31 + n1 1990.

A further extension of this study by Peabody Institute's Dean of the Conservatory of Music examines the relationship of competitions to personal and career development.

Colby, Linda Jenks. "The Rules of Good Page-Turning," *Clavier* 28:30 n2 1989.

Useful "do's" and "don'ts" for those serving as page-turners and/or the pianists in need of their services.

Cooke, James Francis. *Great Pianists on Piano Playing* (Philadelphia: Theodore Presser Co., 1913).

Twenty-eight great pianists of the early twentieth-century (Paderewski, Hofman, etc.) comment on various aspects of the study, teaching, and playing of the piano.

Crowder, Louis. "What is Style?," *Clavier* 5:20–21 + n4 1966.

Discusses variation in style characteristics in playing music of the major composers. Includes suggestions concerning rubato, tempo, pedalling, tone quality, and dynamic range.

Delzell, J.K. "Guidelines for a balanced performance schedule," *Music Educators Journal* 74: 34–38 April, 1988.

Too many performances in school music programs may interfere with real musical learning.

DeVan, William and Carolyn Maxwell. "Preparing Students for Competition," *Clavier* 26:34–36 n4 1987.

Discusses technique, repertoire, experience, and musicianship.

Dubal, David. *Reflections from the Keyboard* (New York: Summit Books, 1984).

A series of interviews with 35 great pianists of the latter twentieth-century (ranging from Claudio Arrau, recently deceased, to the forty-two year old Emmanuel Ax). Davidovich and de Larrocha give interesting insights on the special problems of women performers.

Fenker, Richard. *Stop Studying, Start Learning* (Fort Worth, TX: Tangram Press, 1981).

Techniques for muscle relaxation, positive mental programming, overcoming distractions, and generally improving learning behaviors.

Fishbein, Martin and Susan Middlestadt. "Medical Problems Among ICSOM Musicians: Overview of a National Survey," *Medical Problems of Performing Artists* 3:1–8 March, 1988.

Fully 76% of musicians performing with 48 orchestras reported at least one severe medical performance problem: stage fright was among those most frequently mentioned.

Foldes, Andor. *Keys to the Keyboard: A Book for Pianists* (New York: E.P.Dutton, 1948).

Comments by a mid-century virtuoso on technique, practice, memorizing, performance. Question and answer section.

Foss, Lukas. "The State of Piano Playing in the Twentieth Century," *American Music Teacher* 39:22–23 n1 1989.

Great pianists enter concert careers through love of music, not merely to demonstrate talent and virtuosity.

Freyhan, Michael. "Reaching for the Chamber Music Ideal," *Piano Quarterly* 38:34–37 n151 1990.

Reviews the differences between performing on the piano and on stringed instruments, and suggests ways to improve balance, intonation, and helpful cooperation between the players.

Garniez, Nancy. "The Teacher-Performer," *Piano Quarterly* 21:14–15 n79 1972.

Teachers of beginning as well as advanced students should perform from memory or with music, whichever is more comfortable.

Green, Barry. *The Inner Game of Music* (New York: Anchor Press, 1986).

Techniques for minimizing the "self-interference" of anxiety, fear, and tension, so that full performance potential may be realized.

———. "Gaining Control by Letting Go: The Inner Game of Music," *American Music Teacher* 37:12–15 n3 1988.

Performance anxiety can be reduced by letting go *of* the inner critic and letting go *to* the sounds, imagery, and/or emotion of the music.

Harris, Sandra R. "A Study of Musical Performance Anxiety," *American Music Teacher* 37:15–16 n4 1988.

Survey of music professors finds ten major categories of coping strategies for performance pressures.

Harting, Lynn. "Let Yourself Perform: Confidence-Building Tips," *Music Educators Journal* 72:46–48 September, 1985.

How to avoid self-criticism and judgment during performances.

Horowitz, Joseph. *The Ivory Trade* (New York: Summit Books, 1990).

Detailed history and examination of the Van Cliburn competition, with profiles of the gold medal winners' subsequent lives and careers.

Horowitz, Joseph. "The Ivory Trade," *American Music Teacher* 40:18–21 + n3 1990–91.

Excerpt from book listed above. Suggests that the Cliburn competition could be improved by free choice of solo repertoire; eliminating big prizes; and ceasing to defer to the music businessmen. Winners should not be ranked as art is not quantifiable.

James, I.M., R.M.Pearson, D.M.N.Griffith, *et al.* "Effect of oxprenolol on stage-fright in musicians," *Lancet* 2:952–54, 1977.

Oxprenolol (beta-blocking agent) assessed in 24 string players under stressful conditions was found to lower anxiety and improve musical performance.

Kapell, William. "Technique and Musicianship," *Etude* 68:20–21 December, 1950.

Need for technical work to be made as musical as possible. Also recollections of Olga Samaroff's memorable teaching of musicianship.

Karp, David. "Understanding Performance Anxiety," *Clavier* 27:16–19 n1 1988.

Ten common distortions of thinking that cause pre-performance stress and anxiety.

Liden, S. and C.Gottfries. "Beta-blocking agents in the treatment of catecholamine-induced symptoms in musicians," *Lancet* 2:529, 1974.

Alprenolol (a beta-blocking agent) was found to ameliorate symptoms of performance anxiety in a group of symphony players.

Mach, Elyse. *Great Pianists Speak for Themselves,* Two Volumes (New York: Dodd, Mead, 1980–88).

Statements by two groups of pianists (the second volume includes mostly younger artists) about their pianistic education, philosophies, and lives as performers.

Magrath, Jane. "Nerves, Memory, and Pianos," *American Music Teacher* 32:17–18 n6 1983.

The best remedy for nervousness is concentration on the music during practice and performance.

Manchester, Ralph A. "The Incidence of Hand Problems in Music Students," *Medical Problems of Performing Artists* 3:15–18 December, 1988.

Study of hand problems in university music school performance majors (see Bibliography for Part I above).

Maris, Barbara English. "Points to Ponder When Preparing to Perform," *American Music Teacher* 36:30–31 n5 1987.

Useful check-list of things to do and remember before, during, and after a performance.

Miller, Richard. "Is there a Cure for Performance Anxiety?," *NATS Journal* 45:19–22 n1 1988.

Proper mental set and preparation for performance a preventive to anxiety. Addressed to singers but equally valid for pianists.

Moore, Gerald. *The Unashamed Accompanist* (New York: MacMillan, 1946).

Treats many aspects of an accompanist's work and preparation for this career.

———. *Am I Too Loud?* (New York: MacMillan, 1962).

The personal and professional memoirs of one of the century's leading accompanists.

Mouledous, Alfred. "Mental Practice," *Clavier* 3:38–39 n3 1964.

The goal of natural performance can be achieved by mental concentration on the music, to the exclusion of muscular awareness.

"The Music Clinic," *Lancet* 1:1309–10, 1985.

Hand difficulties of pianists with particular composers' works. Cramps, pain, and weakness are mid-career symptoms, with stiffness more prevalent in the elderly.

Nagel, J., *et al.* "Coping with performance anxiety," *NATS Bulletin* 37:26+ n4 1981.

Cognitive coping skills taught in the University of Michigan Performance Anxiety Program (1978–1980).

Nagel, Louis B. "Overcoming Performance Anxiety," *Clavier* 24:22–23 n7 1985.

Techniques to overcome the chief causes of performance anxiety, namely, possibilities of memory slips and technical collapse.

Newman, William S. *The Pianist's Problems* (New York: Harper & Row, 1950).

Principles of technique, practice, historical styles, and musicianly playing.

Noyle, Linda J. *Pianists On Playing: Interviews with Twelve Concert Pianists* (Metuchen, NJ: Scarecrow Press, 1987).

Author interviews twelve pianists (see Bibliographies for Parts I and II above).

Pierce, Alexandra. "Doing and Overdoing in Performance," *Piano Quarterly* 22:40–41 + n87 1974.

After a piece is securely learned, a performer should relinquish the conscious process (i.e. muscular tension and planning ahead), letting his personal energy merge with the music.

Reubart, Dale. *Anxiety and Musical Performance* (New York: Da Capo Press, 1985).

Exhaustive study of the causes and management of pianistic performance anxiety.

Rutman, Neil. "Do You Have an Image?" *Piano Quarterly* 37:58–61 n144 1988–89.

A moving musical interpretation requires that the performer have an inner image of the music, be it emotional, visual, or programmatic.

Samaroff, Olga. "Accuracy in Musical Performance," *Musical Courier* 149:32–34 n11 1954.

A plea for training piano students toward musical independence in approaching scores of all periods.

Sandor, Gyorgy. *On Piano Playing* (New York: Schirmer Books, 1981).

Details of technique, memorizing, concert performance. Many photographs of hand movements and musical examples.

Schonberg, Harold. *The Great Pianists* (New York: Simon and Schuster, 1987).

An exhaustive history of piano playing from the eighteenth-century to the present, based on written material, recordings, and oral history.

Slenczynska, Ruth. "From Studio to Stage," *Clavier* 7:41–43 n2 1968.

How to get a memorized composition into shape for stage performance.

————. *Music at Your Fingertips* (New York: Da Capo Press, 1974). Originally published 1961.

Practicing, projection, use of tape-recorder, building repertoire and concert programs.

Tollefson, Arthur R. "Debussy's Pedaling," *Clavier* 9:22–33 n7 1970.

Debussy calls for two pedals only: damper, to prolong sound, alter its quality, and effect dynamic emphasis, and una corda, to ensure "understatement" at any level.

Wagner, Jeffrey and Corey Kaup. "Record Yourself at the Piano," *Clavier* 28:17–20 n7 1989.

Recording is a useful tool for audition or teaching purposes. Important factors in a successful product are the room, the piano, the quality of tapes and tape deck, the selection of microphones and their placement.

Whiteaker, C.S. "The modification of psychophysical response to stress in piano performance," *Dissertation Abstracts* 46:1438A-1439A December, 1985.

Performers exposed to a training program containing muscle relaxation and cognitive-behavioral components showed a significant decrease in anxiety levels and increased confidence in performance.

Wolff, Konrad. "About Singing a Melody on the Piano," *Piano Quarterly* 25:49–52 n99 1977.

Piano melodies really have more resemblance to bowed or spoken phrases than to those performed by singers.

Ziporyn, Terra. "Pianist's cramp to stage-fright: the medical side of music-making," *Journal of the American Medical Association* 252:985–89 n8 1984.

Describes a number of physical and psychological problems of performing musicians, and some of the conferences and clinics now being set up to deal with them.

ABOUT THE AUTHOR

RUTH C. FRIEDBERG (A.B., Barnard College; M.A., University of North Carolina) is Director of Music and Professor of Piano at Incarnate Word College in San Antonio, Texas. For twelve years, she was on the music faculty of Duke University and has also taught at the University of Texas and the New School of Music in Philadelphia. She has concertized and given lecture-recitals throughout the United States and Canada, and was the keyboard artist of the San Antonio Symphony from 1976 to 1987. Her articles on twentieth-century music and composers have appeared in many periodicals as well as in the *New Grove's Dictionaries of Music,* and Scarecrow Press has published her three volume *American Art Song and American Poetry,* 1981–87. She has regularly been adjudicator for the piano division of the San Antonio Symphony's Young Artist Competition, and has served as a preliminary judge for the San Antonio International Piano Competition.